DRAMATIC READINGS
ON
FEMINIST ISSUES, Vol I

By Meg Bowman

Sponsored By: Women and Religion Task Force,
A Committee of Pacific Central District
Unitarian Universalist Association

Readings For Women's Programs
Memorial Services For Women
Goddesses, Witches And The Paradigm Shift
Famous Unitarian Universalist Women
   (with Dr. Henry Van Dyke)

DRAMATIC READINGS
ON
FEMINIST ISSUES, Vol. I

Meg Bowman

Hot Flash Press
Box 21506
San Jose, CA 95151

For my beloved granddaughter Christine Ann and her generation: May you never forget your courageous foremothers who paved the way.

Sponsored by:
Women and Religion Task Force, a committee of Pacific Central District
Unitarian Universalist Association

CONTENTS

Meg Bowman teaches sociology at San Jose State University.

A veteran of the 1960s civil rights and peace movements, she is now a feisty feminist who lectures, writes, and leads feminist tours. In 1985, she took a group of over 100 people to Nairobi, Kenya for the U.N. Decade for Women Conference, and in 1987 she led a study group to the Orient.

Known for her innovative teaching, Meg often uses the dramatic reading format in the classroom. These dramatic readings are designed to raise consciousness' and to, hopefully, change the world.

INTRODUCTION

As a feminist, I provide educational and consciousness raising programs for N.O.W. and O.W.L.* meetings, Unitarian Universalist services and Womyn's History Week programs. These often take the form of dramatic readings.

As a teacher, I find dramatic readings a wonderful way to explore history, analyze social problems, and exchange ideas in the college classroom.

These five **Dramatic Readings on Feminist Issues** provide YOU with the tools so that you can put on your own programs. The readings can be used "as is", shortened, or expanded by adding suggested poetry, responsive readings, candlelightings, songs, and/or group discussions. You can enjoy them at a party, or just get some friends together for a play reading.

They are educational consciousness raisers. They are serious and they are fun. They can be rehearsed or read cold. They are about planning the first woman's right conference, sexism in religions, peace, violence, rape, the double standard, patriarchy and the women's liberation movement. They evoke feelings of joy, despair, anger, hope, rage and delight. They deliver messages inherent in Feminism—love, justice, peace, and commitment.

Enjoy!

—Meg Bowman, Ph.D., 1988

*National Organization for Women
Older Women's League

ACKNOWLEDGEMENTS

I am deeply thankful to everyone who contributed to these dramatic readings, particularly Ellen Bass, Ramona Barth, Marylou Hadditt, Bruce Southworth, Pat Stanton, and Charlotte Suskind for their creative writing.

Special thanks to Jean Embree, Jenny Joseph, Betty Mills, Ruth Van Gorder and Ellen Bass for their thought-provoking poetry.

My appreciation also goes to Bulbul, who graciously gave permission to use her insightful cartoon, and to Jenny Grover for her powerful song. I am especially grateful to Carolyn McDade for allowing us to print her inspiring songs.

Sincere thanks to the proofreaders, Trudy Kilian, Lynn Halevi, Gina Allen, Barbara Glass, and Marta Hiatt and to Rosalie Nichols and the other women at Ms. Atlas Press for printing and assembling the manuscript.

A special remembrance to all the students who stood in front of class and read these dramas 'cold,' and to the Militant Menopausal Women of the San Jose Unitarian Church who performed them all over the Bay Area. You are much appreciated.

Never will I forget the cacophony of dozens of reverberating voices as we rehearsed in the huge Kenyatta College cafeteria the evening before presenting three of the dramatic readings at the NGO Forum, United Nation's Decade For Women Conference, Nairobi, Kenya in 1985.

Meg Bowman
Women and Religion Task Force
A Committee of the Pacific Central District,
Unitarian Universalist Association

OUR
STUNNING HARVEST:
DRAMATIC READING

Based on "Our Stunning Harvest"
A poem by ELLEN BASS

Adapted for Dramatic Reading by
MEG BOWMAN

This poem is anti-war.

This poem is anti-violence.

OUR STUNNING HARVEST:
DRAMATIC READING

An adaptation of Ellen Bass' poem "Our Stunning Harvest"
for a cast of seven — four women, two men and a young girl,
plus a voice in the audience.

anti-war
anti-rape
anti-violence

This anti-war, anti-rape, anti-violence dramatic reading requires
only one read-through before performing.

Memorizing is not necessary.

No props are needed.

Your program can be twenty minutes long or expanded to a full
hour.

You may concentrate on an anti-war theme, or include the
anti-rape material, thus tying violence-against-women to war.

Design your own program: In addition to the dramatic reading, a
poem, a reading on violence, two responsive readings, and six of
Carolyn McDade's songs are included.

ACKNOWLEDGEMENTS

Ellen Bass graciously gave permission to print her poem "Our Stunning Harvest" as a Dramatic Reading. This powerful poem is from her book *Our Stunning Harvest and Other Poems* (Moving Parts Press and New Society Publishers, 1984).

Ellen is the author of several collections of poetry, e.g. *For Earthly Survival* (Moving Parts Press, Santa Cruz, 1980); *I'm Not Your Laughing Daughter* (U. of Mass. Press, 1973); *Of Separateness and Merging* (Autumn Press, 1977); *Haiti: August 13-28* (Out of Sight Books, 1977); *For Earthy Survival* (Moving Parts Press, 1980); and she co-edited with Florence Howe *No More Masks: An Anthology of Poems By Women* (Doubleday/Anchor, 1973). She co-edited with Louise Thornton *I Never Told Anyone: Writings by Women Survivors of Child Sexual Abuse* (Harper & Row, 1983).

Ellen, who lives in Santa Cruz, CA and travels nationally teaching writing workshops for women as well as leading groups for women survivors of child sexual abuse, kindly gave permission to print her poem, "Women and Children First."

Carolyn McDade enthusiastically gave permission to print several of her songs. Currently writing new songs at Womanspace Center, Plainville, Mass., Carolyn will soon be on another concert tour. Watch for announcements of her concerts in your area; she is wonderful!

Heartfelt thanks to Katherine Oppenheimer, Sunnyvale, CA for graphics, Cleo Kocol, Seattle, WA for editing suggestions, and Trudy Kilian, San Jose, CA for proof-reading.

Each of you sensitive, talented women are part of the world-wide peace movement shouting NO MORE WAR!

Meg Bowman, 1987

TABLE OF CONTENTS

> "You can no longer save your family, tribe or nation anymore.
> You can only save the whole world."
> — Dr. Margaret Mead

PRODUCTION NOTES

1. No props are necessary, but you will need someone to turn the lights up or on/and down or off. This person will need a copy of the script.

2. The cast need not memorize their roles; one read-through is usually enough before a performance.

3. When not reading, cast members should look at the person *who is reading* and *not* down at their script.

4. The child's age may vary between six and ten and the script has been adapted to reflect this. If the girl does not yet read, she will have four lines to memorize; the mother may press the child's shoulder as a signal for her to speak her lines. If the child can read, type the four lines on a 5" x 7" card for her to hold.

5. If there are several children in your audience, you may wish to invite them to sit in front, on the stage, or near the cast.

6. Introduce the members of the cast at the end of the dramatic reading.

You can't hug your child with nuclear arms.

OUR STUNNING HARVEST: DRAMATIC READING

CAST:

Mother .... Female
Father .... Male
Child .... Female
Reader #1 .... Female
Reader #2 .... Female
M.D. (husband of reader #2) .... Male
Voice in audience .... Female

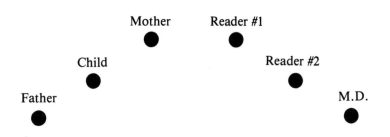

Mother   Reader #1

Child

Reader #2

Father   M.D.

Audience

◆ ◆ ◆ ◆ ◆

OUR STUNNING HARVEST: DRAMATIC READING

PROGRAM OPTIONS:

1. This program can be adapted to a classroom, used as a church program, presented before a meeting or gathering of an organization, such as WILPF, N.O.W., LWV, AAUW, NWPC — I, for example, have used it in sociology classes, before the National Institute of Humanist Counselors, AHA, for a N.O.W. film festival, as a Unitarian Sunday morning church service, etc.

2. Feel free to create your own program, e.g.

    (1) Use only the dramatic reading which will take about twenty minutes.

    (2) Develop a full one-hour program with song(s), poem(s), a reading on violence, a dramatic reading, and end with a responsive reading and a song. If possible, lead a discussion on violence and the future after the program. (See Suggested Program, p. 11)

    (3) Use only the anti-war theme and delete all material on rape; to do this, omit all lines with an (*) asterisk in front of them in the dramatic reading, and exclude other materials on rape.

    (4) Open your program with Holly Near's recording of the song, "No, no don't melt into one" (from *Singing For Our Lives*, Holly Near, Redwood Records, Oakland, CA, 1982). Other Holly Near songs you might consider using are "No More Genocide in My Name" and "Watch Out" from her 1984 album of the same title.

    (5) Begin your program by having a guitarist play and sing familiar peace songs, e.g. "Let There Be Peace On Earth," "Where Have All the Young Men Gone?"

    Also, soft guitar music playing familiar peace songs can be played intermittently in the background throughout the dramatic reading.

(6) Read a poem *before* the dramatic reading, e.g. if you include the rape material:

"(Today/Tonight) we bring you an anti-war, anti-rape, anti-violence program. Rape is an act of violence — an act of anger, of power. Marge Piercy writes . . . " (Read the first four stanzas of "Rape Poem" by Marge Piercy, *Circle on the Waters: Selected Poems of Marge Piercy* (Alfred A. Knopf, 1982, p. 164).

Or, if your major theme is anti-war:

"(Today/Tonight) we bring you an anti-violence program. The ultimate violence is war. Here is Ellen Bass' poem 'Women and Children First'." (See p. 12)

(7) Have your audience, a quartette, choir, soloist . . . sing as many peace songs as you wish. (Six of Carolyn McDade's songs are on pp. 37-42.)

(8) Play one or more peace songs on cassette, e.g. *We Come With Our Voices, Songs of Carolyn McDade With Friends* (1982), Surtsey Publishing, 111 Mt. Vernon Street, Newtonville, MA 02160, or *Swords into Plowshares*, Pythagoras Press, Box 1153, Carmel Valley, CA 93924, 408/659-2086. $10 ppd.

(9) When using a responsive reading (such as "We, The People of The World" (see p. 35), or "World Beyond War" (see p. 36), be sure that your audience has copies.

Responsive readings may, of course, be read as prose by one person.

(10) If desired, copies of this reading can be made available to your audience so that they may follow the script as it is being performed. (Write for quantity discount prices.)

3. After the performance, give your audience an opportunity to do something constructive to reduce violence in our world, e.g. offer a petition to be signed, pass out stationery and envelopes and have people write letters to elected representatives, collect

money for a Rape Crisis Center or a peace project, and/or make an announcement of a forthcoming Peace March, Peace Vigil, Peace Program, etc.

4. This program invites discussion. Time permitting, open discussion by asking the people in your audience a question, e.g. "Do you feel optimistic or pessimistic regarding the future of our planet?"

— mb

It's a man's world unless women vote.

A SUGGESTED PROGRAM

Welcome . . . . (Name)

Song: "Call to Women," Carolyn McDade, led by . (Name)
(See p. 37)

Reading on Violence . . . . (Name)
(See p. 13)

Poem: "Women and Children First," Ellen Bass . . . (Name)
(See p. 12)*

Dramatic Reading: "OUR STUNNING HARVEST"
An adaptation of Ellen Bass' poem "Our Stunning Harvest"
(See pp. 17-34)

Cast:

Mother . . . . (Name)
Father . . . . (Name)
Reader #1 . . . . (Name)
Reader #2 . . . . (Name)
M.D. . . . . (Name)
Voice in Audience . . . . (Name)
Child . . . . (Name)

Responsive Reading: "We, The People of The World"
Led by . . . . (Name)
(See p. 35)

Song: "Coming Home," Carolyn McDade, led by . (Name)
(See p. 40)

*If material on rape is included in your program, you may wish to add "Rape Poem" by Marge Piercy (see #6, p. 9).

Women and Children First

They used to protect us
if a ship sunk
if a building caught fire,
even in war though they raped us, they
usually let us live.

We couldn't own land
sit on juries, heal with herbs
or go to school

but they did recognize
we were necessary.

Now barrels of plutonium
leak in the ocean, seep underground,
cores of radioactive ore
lie about like sand piles, accidents
that couldn't happen
happen.

Most susceptible are the young:
children, babies, babies in our wombs,
Women and children first.

— Ellen Bass

READING ON VIOLENCE
(for beginning of program)

We know we live in a violent society. The history of the United States is a history of violence. The genocide of Native Americans. Slavery and racism. Lynchings and sexism. Nativism and Nationalism. We have a history of macho Saturday night entertainment of rape and gang bangs, burning down Chinatowns, beating up "the old lady," and shoot-outs with Saturday night specials. And wars.

We reap a bitter harvest. We have the highest crime rate and the highest homicide rate in the world.

In the United States, in the next 50 minutes, there will be 200 women beaten by men they know; men they live with. On the average, a woman is battered every fifteen seconds; over 1.8 million women beaten each year. In the next 50 minutes, 167 women will be raped; on the average, a woman is raped every eighteen seconds; sixty-five men and women will be assaulted; fifty-one homes and businesses will be broken into and robbed. In the next 50 minutes, 190 children will be beaten. A conservative estimate is that two million children become victims of child abuse each year. Some research indicates the number to be over six million. Over 5,000 die as a result of such abuse. Physical abuse and neglect, sexual abuse, emotional abuse and the problems continue to grow. In the next 50 minutes, 100 children will be sexually abused; one in every 5 victims is a child under the age of seven. In the next 50 minutes, four people will be killed, one by a member of their family, another by someone they know.

Violence is learned behavior. By age 14, the average child in the United States has witnessed over 27,000 murders on television and seen over 200,000 other acts of violence. As many as 2,000 parents are killed by their children each year. Nationwide, researchers estimate one in ten parents are attacked by their children each year.

And the ultimate crime? Destroying the entire planet with acid rain, pesticides, Agent Orange, polluting the water, lakes, wells, oceans. The polluting is so subtle, so insidious: We throw away one little cigarette butt, one little plastic bag . . . it all adds up. Companies in Silicon Valley,* the cutting edge of Toffler's 'Third Wave,' have seeped toxic chemicals into public water supplies so that dozens of wells are now closed. We can destroy our planet gradually . . . or quickly. All life is threatened by nuclear holocaust. World suicide. A dead planet. Nuclear winter. In the next 50 minutes, this nation will spend over $60 million on war. We spend over $1 million per minute on bigger and better ways to blow up the world. In 1983, the General Accounting Office reported that the Reagan military program would cost $2.25 trillion over the next five years.

Violence — from rape to nuclear war. Violence — from battered women to the manufacture of lethal gasses and germ warfare cannisters. It's all related. Show women as body parts in pornography and women become targets for violence — rape, battery, molest, homicide. It's all related. Power. Anger. Misogyny. M-X Missiles (now officially called 'the peace keepers'), Cruise Missiles. Nuclear stockpiling. Over-kill. My gun is bigger than your gun. A man's home is his castle, and don't you forget it! Mucho macho hierarchical patriarchy . . . the world held hostage. The media glorifies it. In fact, most people cannot even imagine a world of peace — a world of plenty — a world without hierarchies of power.

Our children may *not* grow up. The world may very well be destroyed by those in power — in Congress, in the Oval office, the politburo, the Pentagon. Everything people have created through the eons — gone. OUR STUNNING HARVEST.

*Santa Clara County, California.

So Must Peace Come

So must peace come
not by the momentous
stroke of pen on paper -
a peace treaty,
an arms limitation,
a nuclear freeze -
but slowly, silently,
from every inner heart
whose prayer for peace
is a nugget of gold
dropped into the center
of the world's desire.
The ripples move
into wider and ever wider
circles until one day
they will have reached
around the earth and come
again to their beginning.
Then peace will cover
the earth and the seas
and reach into the farthest
eternities of space.

So must peace come
from the heart of everyone.

-Elizabeth Searle Lamb

CAST OPTIONS:

Cast can begin with bent backs, strained necks, arms wrapped tight around torsos. As the Dramatic Reading evolves, heads can be thrown back, mouths open and singing, bare feet stomping the earth, arms thrown wide in embrace. Or, cast can stand throughout the performance, stepping forward only when speaking.

INTRODUCTION

Cast stands with their backs to the audience. Lights up as one person turns to face the audience and reads.

OUR STUNNING HARVEST: DRAMATIC READING

This poem is a dance. This poem is a sustained wail. This poem is of violence —* (the violence of rape and —) the violence of war. It catches in our throats and the pain is never abandoned — even as it is transcended in the final healing vision.

This poem is the color of blood, the color of death, the color of hope and healing. It is the color of rape and the color of bombs, the color of little girls' sneakers and of baby blankets.

Ellen Bass, the author, believes that Part III of this poem should be copied and sent to all the government officials and the pentagon officials and the nuclear power plant officials. It should be memorized and droned by wise old women, acted out of street corners by troops of wandering minstrels, sung by choruses of chest-beating, angry, women-loving women. It should be crooned the way Holly Near tearfully croons over and over, "No, no don't melt into one, / No, no, no, no don't melt into one."

Reader joins cast, turning her/his back to the audience. Lights down.

Delete all material on rape if your program theme is exclusively war/peace.

OUR STUNNING HARVEST: DRAMATIC READING

PART I

Entire cast — except **M.D.** *— turns to face audience.*

Reader #1: She recognized miner's lettuce
nibbles its round leaf.

Her father asks

Father: Do you know
not to eat the other plants?

Reader #1: and she nods solemnly.
(CHILD *nods head*)

Father: We have taught her not to swallow pits
of cherries or olives.
She spits them out bald
and repeats:

Child: Could make a child sick.

Father: And walking, when we hear a car
she runs to the side of the road
stands, stationary, until it passes.

Mother: But how do I protect her
from men who rape children?

Reader #1: from poison in the air?

Reader #2: from nuclear holocaust?

Mother: I walk this road — oak trees, eucalyptus
                blackberry bushes in white flower
                the hard green fruit pushing out behind the blossoms —
                the first time I have walked here alone
                since the day (a few) years ago
                when I carried her in my belly,
                the morning before her birth.

Father: It was dustier then, drought
                the smell of hot clay and stillness
                in the tall Queen Anne's lace.

Mother: Today the breeze is cool.
                But the dread, the urgency
                etch my pleasure like acid.

                I clean house, shove socks and shirts
                in the washer, speed through the grocery,
                type, fold, staple —
                but what good are dishes stacked in the cupboard,
                peaches and avocados in the basket, envelopes
                stamped in the dark mailbox?

                At night I lie in bed imagining
                    what I will do if† attacked
              *alone, I could run
              *or fight
              *but with her . . . holding my hand
              *on this country road?

†If using *primarily the peace theme*, delete "attacked," substitute
" . . . there is nuclear war" and add "I could run, but where?"

*If your theme is only world peace, delete lines having to do with
rape (those with an asterisk in front of them).*

*A mother bird flutters and distracts.
*She risks her life, but the babies are protected.
*I could not even protect her.
*She is too small to run. If I whispered "run"
*she would not go. And if I tried to carry her
*we would be overcome. I could not fight with her
*in my arms. Far from help, I am prey.
*With her as hostage
*I am blackmailed.
*And if I am not enough? if they want her too?

My husband sleeps by my side
his regular sleep breath. I
lean closer, try to absorb
the calm. But the possibilities do not stop.

I don't let them. I keep trying scenarios,
*get as far as convincing the rapist to let me
        take her to a neighbor
*then rushing into the house, locking him out.
*But he may not even speak English
*I sober myself, and besides . . .

I am sick in the night, sick in the day.
My stomach won't digest food,
    it runs through me, foul, waste.
By noon I fall asleep,
    she sleeps in the crook of my arm.
We sleep for hours. For these few hours
    we are safe.
I know we have been safe
    afterward.

Cast turns their backs to audience. Lights dim. Pause.

Delete all material on rape if your program theme is exclusively war/peace.

PART II

Lights up. All readers face the audience.

Reader #2: Yesterday I read they tried to kill Dr. Rosalie Bertell,
a nun who researched radiation-caused cancer.

Reader #1: Here, the resource center for nonviolence is shot up,
tires slashed.

Reader #2: My husband is limiting his practice
so he can work against nuclear destruction.
He says,

M.D.: We may be in danger, you know.
If the steering on the car ever feels funny
pull right over.

Reader #2: He's had the lug nuts loosened before.

M.D.: But we both know that is not the greatest danger.
Radiation from Lovecreek, Churchrock, Rocky Flats,
Three Mile Island, West Valley, Hanford —
we live near the San Andreas Fault —
an earthquake
and the Diablo Canyon plant
could kill millions —
and bombs, the Trident, the MX Missiles —
the draft beginning again.

Reader #2: Who are these madmen
whose lives are so barren, so desperate
they love nothing?

Reader #1: What will it take to make them change?

Mother: What will it take?

Reader #2: What will it take to make *me* change?
I still use plastic bags from Dow Chemical.
When am I
going to stop?

M.D.: *Polyvinylchloride poisons your food.*

Reader #2: What do you do with *your* lettuce?
Glass jars, or a pot with a lid?

Reader #1: *(smiles)* I have a pot with a lid.

Reader #2: What good will one woman
never again using plastic bags do
in the face of tons of plutonium, recombinant DNA
*a hundred thousand rapists?

Mother: What good does it do that I feed my daughter organic
rice, purple beets, never sugar?

Reader #1: What good that I march with other women
and we yell WOMEN UNITED
WILL NEVER BE DEFEATED *(repeat)*
banshees into the night?

Mother: These things can not save my daughter.
I know. I know that.
But unless I do them
she will not be saved.

and I want to save her.
Oh Mother of us all, I am a mother too
I want to save her.

(Cast turn their backs to audience. Pause as lights dim.)

*Substitute "DDT, EDB, Strontium 90 . . . ?"

PART III

(Only READER #1 *turns and steps center stage. Lights up.)*

Reader #1: I want to talk to the president.
I want to go with other mothers
and meet with the president.
And I want mothers from Russia there.
And the head of Russia.
And Chinese mothers
and the head of China
and mothers from Saudi Arabia and Japan
and South Africa
and the heads of state and the families of the heads of
state and the children, all the children of the mothers.

Mother: *(Turns face to audience.)*
I want a meeting.
I want to ask the president, *Is there nothing
precious to you?*

Reader #1: And when the president explains how it's the
Russians, I want the Russian women to say *We don't
want war.* I want all the women to scream

All: *(Rest of cast faces audience and shouts)*
WE DON'T WANT WAR, WE,
THE PEOPLE, DO NOT WANT WAR.

M.D.: And I want the president to admit he wants war,
he wants power and money and war more
than he wants the lives of his children.
I want to see him turn to his children and tell them
they will not live, that
no one will live,
that with one computer error all life on this planet can

be annihilated, that two men could go mad
and push one button
in a silo, in a plane, that these men do go mad,
are replaced, that one
might not be replaced soon enough.

Father: I want each head of state to tell his children
what will happen
if any country sent a thermonuclear bomb.
I want each head of state, with his own tongue,
to tell his children
how the computers of the other country
would pick up the signal,
how they would fire back, how the bombs would hit.

M.D.:   I want each president and prime minister and king
to tell his children how firestorms would burn,
vaporizing people,
animals, plants, and then as days passed,
how the millions would die of radiation sickness,
their skins sloughing off, the nausea, hair falling out,
hemorrhage, infection, no hospitals, no clean water,
the stench of dead and decaying bodies,
bacteria, and virus rampant,
insects rampant, and the radiation ticking, ticking
as millions more die over the next years, leukemia,
cancer and no hope for the future,
birth deformity, stillbirth, miscarriage, sterility,
millions and billions.

Mother: I want them to watch the faces of their children.
I want them to watch their eyes pale
the flecks of light fading,
and when their children ask

Child: Why? Why?

Mother: I want them to point to the other heads of state
and the others to point back
and I want the mothers screaming.
I want the mothers of the children of the heads of state
screaming.

I want them to scream until their voices are hoarse
        whispers
raw as the bloody rising of the sun, I want them to hiss

Reader #1: How dare you?

Reader #2: How dare you?

Mother: Kill them yourself, then.

Father: Kill them here, now, with your own hands.

M.D.:   Kill all these children, clench
           your hands around their necks, crunch their spines.

Voice in   Kill one
Audience: two, three, kill hundreds. If you are going to kill
           then kill.

Mother: I want to see the faces of the president, the premier,
               the prime minister, the chancellor, the king.
           I want to see their faces tremble.
           I want to see them tremble
               like a still lake under wind.
           I want to see them weep.

Reader #2: I must be crazy myself.
           My mother is an optimist. She believes in a
               "survival instinct."
           She has read the statistics, knows
           Plutonium is poison for 500,000 years.
           But she does not think of these things.
           It depresses her, she says.

Voice in
Audience: I say she is naive.

Reader #1: But I write poems in which presidents
               and premiers weep
           at the voices of raging mothers. I write,
           they weep.
           I must be crazy.

And I want this meeting like a crazy woman wants.

Mother: I want to go myself.
           I want my daughter to ride her
              four-wheeled horse (or bicycle) around the
              carpeted room, fast, steering with
              her red sneakered feet,
           through potted plants and filing cabinets,
           precise, dauntless.
           I want her spirit to inspire us.
           I don't want to hear about numbers.
           I don't want to hear one number
           about how many bombs or
              how much money or dates or
              megatons or anything else.
           I want to hear

All: NO MORE.

Mother: I want to hear

All: MY CHILD WILL NOT BE MURDERED.
           MY CHILD WILL LIVE.

Mother: I want to dance victorious, to dance and dance
           ring around the rosie, with no one falling down.
           No ashes, no ashes.
           I want no ashes from my child's tender head.
           I want to dance. I want to sing. I want to kiss all
              the heads of state, all the mothers, every child.
           I want to kiss them all and dance the hora, dance the
              mazurka, the waltz, the tribal dances, bare feet on
              red clay
              on white sand
              on black earth.

(If desired, MOTHER *and* child *can dance in a circle.)*

Reader #2: dancing, kissing, singing
dancing, dancing until our legs are strong
our arms strong, our thighs, lungs, bellies strong,
until our voices are loud, clear, and vibrate with the
    wind
until we ride the wind
until we ride home, with the wind, flying, flying
laughing, kissing, singing, cackling, our children
tucked under our wings, safe.

Father: Safe. We are safe. We are so strong.
          We *can* protect our children.

(Cast turns back to audience. Lights dim. Pause.)

PART IV

Voice
from
Audience: No you won't!

(Lights up. Cast turns to face audience.)

Reader #1: The (young) composed woman taunts us . . .

Reader #2: No, she is our teacher.
           She is teaching us our power.
           We must yell back —

Voice: No you won't.

All: YES WE WILL!

Voice: No you won't.

All: YES WE WILL. YES WE WILL!

Voice: Say, "Yes I will."

All: Yes, I will.

Voice: AGAIN!

All: YES I WILL. YES I WILL. YES, I WILL!

Reader #2: *(trembling voice)* Yes I will.

Mother: I will.
           I will protect my daughter.

Father: How
           will I protect my daughter?

Reader #1: *Even if we dismantle the bombs,
               cement the power plants,
           *ban 2, 4, 5-T, men are still raping women.

Reader #2: *Men raped women before they split the atom
           *before they concocted herbicides
               in their stainless steel
               laboratories.
           *They raped in war and they raped
               in what they call peace,
           *they raped in marriage.

Reader #1: *they raped in groups, they raped old
               women, young women,
           *they raped when they were angry,
               they raped when they were scorned,
           *they raped when they got drunk,
               got high, got a weekend
               pass, got on the Dean's list, got fired.

M.D.:   *They still do.

Mother: *They rape women asleep, children asleep —
               fathers have easy access to children asleep.

M.D.:   *They rape babies —
               doctors treat three-month-old babies for gonorrhea
               of the throat.

Reader #1: *They rape women getting into their cars after late
            night shifts,

Reader #2: *they rape old women washing up
            their breakfast dishes.

Mother: *they call on the phone and threaten rape.

Father: *they write songs like *your lips tell me no no, but
            there's yes yes in your eyes,*

Mother: *they design high heeled sandals so we can't run away,

Reader #1: *they invented the pill — easy sex
            and we die from cancer
            when they're done.

Reader #2: *They use knives and guns when subtler
            coercion is not
            enough,

Reader #1: *sometimes they use the knives and guns anyway,
            afterward.

Mother: And how shall I protect her?

All: How shall we protect each other?

Mother: *I can warn her not to talk to strangers
            *I can forbid her to go out at night.

Father: *I can nag her to press her knees together
            and button her blouse to her neck,
            *but none of that will assure her safety
            *or even her survival.

Mother: *I can enroll her in self-defense, judo, karate,
            *I can practice with her in our yard. We can grow
            *quick and deft, together.

Father: *And that will help, but it is not enough.
             *Three boys with razor blades, a man with a 45 . . .

Reader #1: *We can castrate rapists. My mother suggested that.
             *She thinks simply, and frankly, I like the idea.

Reader #2: *But the damage is already done, and the next time
             *they can use a broken bottle, it's not sex they want.

All: So what's enough? what's enough?

Reader #1: Only
             to gather
             to gather as our foremothers gathered.

Reader #2: Wild plants, berries, nuts — they were gathered.
             They gathered together, their food,
                their sustenance —
             reeds for weaving baskets, feathers,
                raven and flamingo
             dyes, ochre and vermillion.

M.D.:   They gathered flat stones for pounding
             scooped stones for grinding; they gathered rocks,
             they gathered shells and the meat of the shells —
             conch, mussel, clam.

Father: They gathered wood for fire.

Mother: They gathered clay from the riverbank
             they kneaded the clay, they pinched and pressed it
             with their fingers
             they shaped bowls and jars,
             they baked the vessels in the coals of the fire.

Reader #1: They gathered water, they gathered rain,
             they gathered honey, they gathered the stories
             of their mothers —
             their grandmothers.

Reader #2: They gathered under moonlight:
they danced, the feel of cool packed dirt under feet
they sang praises, they cried prayers.

Reader #1: When attacked, they knew how
to gather their fingers
into a fist . . .

Reader #2: They could jab with sharpened sticks,
they could hurl rock.

Reader #1: They gathered their strength,
they gathered together . . .

Reader #2: They gathered the blessings of the goddess,
their faith in the turning of the earth,
the seasons bleeding into each other
leaves crumbling into earth, earth
sprouting water-green leaves.

Reader #1: They gathered leaves, chickweed, comfrey,
plantain, nettles . . .

Reader #2: They worked together, they fought together.

Mother: They fed, they bathed, they suckled their young.

Father: They gathered stars into constellations
and their reflections into shallow bowls of water . . .

M.D.: They gathered an acknowledged, familiar harmony
one I have never known, one I long for
long to gather
with all you women.

Reader #1: Oh, Women, † I want
to gather with you.
Our numbers are grand.

_____

†You may wish to substitute the word, "People."

Our hands are capable, practiced,
our minds know pattern, know
relationship, how the tree
pulls water up through root
through trunk, through branch, stem
into leaf, how the surface stomata release
water vapor into the air, the air cooled.

Reader #2: We know
to honor trees.
We know
the chrysalis, the grub, the earthworm.

Mother: We women have handled baby poop and vomit —
the incontinence of the old and sick.

Reader #2: We smell menses every month
from the time we are young girls.

Reader #1: We do not faint.
We do not titter
at mice.

Reader #2: We have handled horses, tractors,
scalpels, saws.

Reader #1: We have handled money
and the lack of it
and we have survived.

Reader #2: We have survived
poverty, childbirth fever
forceps, scopolamine
footbindings, excision, infibulation
beatings, thorazine, diet pills
rape, witch burning, valium, chin lifts
female infanticide, child molestation
breast x-rays, suttee.

Reader #1: Some of us have died.

Reader #2:   Millions, millions have been killed,
             murdered.

Reader #1:   We mourn, we mourn
             their courage, their innocence
             their wisdom often lost to us.

Reader #2:   We remember.

Reader #1:   We are fierce
             like a cornered animal.

Reader #2:   Our fury spurts like geysers
             like volcanoes, brilliant lava, molten gold
             cascading in opulent plumes.

Child: And every morning we gather eggs from the chickens
             we milk the goat

Mother: or drive to the Safeway and push our cart
             under fluorescent lights.

Father: We feed our children.

Mother: We feed them blood from our womb
             milk from our breast.
             Our bodies create and nourish life.

Reader #2:   We create. Alone
             we are able to create.

M.D.:   *Parthenogenesis*. Two eggs unite. It happens.

Reader #2:   It has always happened.
             One woman, alone, can create life.

Reader #1:   Think what all of us could do

Reader #2:   if we gather
             gather like the ocean gathers for the wave
             the clouds gather for the storm

Mother: the uterus gathers for contraction
            the pushing out, the birth.

Reader #2: We can gather
            We can save our earth.

Mother: We can labor like we labored
            to birth our babies,
            laboring past thirst, past the rising and the setting
                of the sun

Reader #2: past distraction, past demands
            past the need to pee, to cry, or even to live
            into the consuming pain
                pain
            pain beyond possibility,

Reader #1: until there is nothing but the
            inevitable gathering
            gathering, gathering

Mother: and
            the new is born,
            relief spreading through us
            like the wave after creating
            spreads over sand in a shush of foam, grace
            our saving grace.

(Cast turns their backs to the audience. Pause. Lights dim.)

PART V

(Only FATHER,   MOTHER *and* CHILD *turn to face the audience. Lights up.)*

Father: NO *touch bee*
            (or if an older child: Don't touch the bee.*)*

Child: BITE *my finger*
            (or: It bit my finger.*)*

Father: my daughter explains to me
pulling back her hand from
    the wild mustard blossoms.
    buzzing with furry bees.

Mother: My child
with your neck still creased in slight folds
the tiny white hairs of your back
    stemming up your spine
you *may* live
you *may*, you *may*, oh I want to believe it is possible
that you may live
to handle bees, pick miner's lettuce
eat black olives in the sun,
    to gather
      with me
        with your daughters
          with all the world's life-sweet women,
            OUR STUNNING HARVEST.

WE, THE PEOPLE OF THE WORLD

We, the people of the world, are determined —

> TO SAVE SUCCEEDING GENERATIONS
> FROM THE SCOURGE OF WAR.

We, the people of the world, are determined —

> TO REAFFIRM FAITH IN FUNDAMENTAL
> HUMAN RIGHTS.

We, the people of the world, are determined —

> TO ENSURE THE DIGNITY AND WORTH
> OF THE HUMAN PERSON.

We, the people of the world, are determined —

> TO ENSURE THE EQUAL RIGHTS
> OF WOMEN AND MEN
> OF RICH AND POOR
> THE STRONG AND THE WEAK.

We, the people of the world, are determined —

> TO PROMOTE JUSTICE AND RESPECT
> IN THE RELATIONS OF NATION TO NATION,
> LARGE AND SMALL.

We, the people of the world, are determined —

> TO PROMOTE THE ECONOMIC AND SOCIAL
> ADVANCEMENT OF ALL PEOPLES.
> TO SECURE THESE ENDS, WE,
> THE PEOPLE OF THE UNITED STATES,
> UNITE WITH ALL PEOPLE OF THE WORLD,
> FOR WE ARE DETERMINED
> TO PUT AN END TO WAR.

Blessed Be.

Dear People...
I want to shake you out of
your psychic numbing!

— Dr. Helen Caldicott

WORLD BEYOND WAR

Here on this beautiful planet —
>   THERE IS AN ABUNDANCE OF LIFE.

And among the many species
  there is humankind —
>   A MIRACLE OF CONSCIOUSNESS,
>   WITH UNDISPUTED DOMINION
>   OVER ALL.

With the human brain —
>   WE HAVE CREATED
>   TECHNOLOGICAL TRIUMPHS.

Unlocking the secrets
  of the sun and the atom —
>   HAS GIVEN US UNPRECEDENTED POWER
>   FOR LIFE OR FOR DEATH.

Two paths lie clearly before us:
>   CONTINUED VIOLENCE AND WAR
>   UNLEASHED BY FEAR AND HATRED:

Or — tolerance, understanding
  and cooperation —
>   INSPIRED BY A VISION
>   OF A WORLD BEYOND WAR.

The hope for the continuance of life —
>   LIES WITH HUMAN BEINGS
>   AND OUR ABILITY TO CHANGE
>   THE WAY WE THINK.

We must reach out and find others
  who share our concern —
>   AND WHO WISH
>   TO BRING ABOUT
>   A WORLD BEYOND WAR.

Blessed Be.

We must live together as Sisters and Brothers or perish together as fools.

— M.L. King

Call to Women

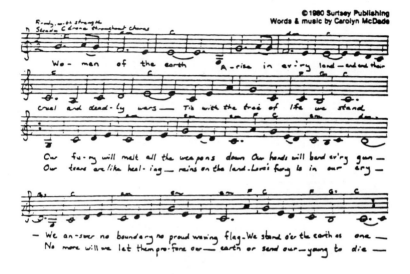

We stand as sisters unto the earth
    her forests of living green
The cypress and ginkgo, the oak and the pine
    the millions unnamed, unseen

Our blood's in the seas pulsing on every shore
    the wind bears our word and our song
So tender our step oh this green growing earth
    that carries life on and on

We're firm as the mountains, as free as the wind,
    as wild as the forest of old
The rights of each generation to come
    unite us with spirits bold

So fierce is our love of this life that we share
    these wars then must wither and cease
Replaced by a justice for one and for all,
    created by living peace

All songs from **Songs by Carolyn McDade**, Surtsey Publishing, 1982.
Endorsed by the Unitarian Universalist Women's Federation.

Published with Carolyn McDade's permission.

Creation of Peace

© 1979 Surtsey Publishing
Music by Carolyn McDade
Words adapted from an address by Barbara Zanotti
at the Riverside Disarmament Conference. She
has breathed a renewed prophetic life into Isaiah & Amos

We'll build a land where we bind up the bro-ken — We'll build a
We'll build a land where we bring — good tid-ings to all the af-
We'll be a land building up an-cient cities — Rais — ing up
Come build a land-where man-tles of prais-es re-sound from —

land where the cap-tives go free. Where the oil of glad-ness dis-solves all
flicted and those — who mourn, we'll then give them garlands in-stead of
dev — as-ta-tions from old. Re — stor-ing ru-ins of gen-er-
spi-rits are faint and are weak. Where like oaks of right-eous-ness stand her

mourning oh we'll build a pro-   mised land that can be.
ashes oh we'll build a land where peace — is born.
a - tions oh we'll be a land — of peo-ple so bold.
peo-ple oh, come build the land — my sis-ters we seek.
(people)

Come build a land where sis-ters and broth-ers: An-oint-ed by

God then cre - ate peace where jus-tice shall roll —

down like waters and peace like an ev — er flow-ing stream.

With Whom Do You Stand?

With those despised, the focus of lies
   who know what it's like to be banned,
Or those who decide who's on the right side,
   Sister, Brother, with whom do you stand?

There're hawks and doves, there's hatred and love,
   there's peace and violence at hand,
There's so much at stake in each choice that we make,
   Sister, Brother, with whom do you stand?

Coming Home

© 1980 Surtsey Publishing
Words & music by Carolyn McDade

Bearing words born new unto each day
Speaking bold where only silence lay
As we dare to rise and lead the way
  We're coming home, we're coming home

As the full moon waxes into wane
Changing, yielding all that she did gain
As from death she dares be born again
  We're coming home, we're coming home

To reclaim the thinking of our minds
Leaving shackles lying far behind
Bearing hope for every soul confined
  We're coming home, we're coming home

To create a world of joy and peace
Where the power of justice does release
Love abounding, wars forever cease
  We're coming home, we're coming home

Peace At Last

Words & music by Carolyn McDade

Peace at last — Peace at last — Put my
hands to peace at last — Peace at last
Peace at last — Fill my soul with peace at last.

Just one world, just one world
Put my hands to just one world
Just one world, just one world
   Fill my soul with just one world

Justice for all, justice for all
Put my hands to justice for all
Justice for all, justice for all
   Fill my soul with justice for all

Joy and love, joy and love
Put my hands to joy and love
Joy and love, joy and love
   Fill my soul with joy and love

What I Do I Do For You

Words & Music by Carolyn McDade

the earth lays brown beneath my feet
  and holds the grasses green and sweet
she holds you and she holds me
  and all the rivers running to the sea

so after all is said and done
  we share the earth, we share the sun
when the moon comes out at night
  she drops her silver light on all alike

as sisters in one family
  the sun, the moon, and you and me
the wind that blows, the grass that grows
  each precious life that comes to live, then goes

WHY WE BURN:

SEXISM EXORCISED

A
Dramatic Reading
On
Sexism in Religion

By
MEG BOWMAN

The Grecian ladies counted their age from their marriage, not their birth.

—Homer
850? B.C.E.

Let women stay at home and hold their peace.
—Aeschylus
Seven Against Thebes, 1.201 (467 B.C.E.)

It is not for women to give counsel.
—Aeschylus (467 B.C.E.)

A woman will bear any weight if it's placed upon her by a man.
—Aristophanes
The Knight, 1, 1056 (424 B.C.E.)

Let your women keep silence in the churches.
—I Corinthians, xiv, 34

Man's work lasts till set of sun
Woman's work is never done.
—Unknown
known in 1655

Howe'er man rules is science and in art,
The sphere of woman's glories is the hart.
—Thomas Moore,
Epilogue to the Tragedy of Ina, 1, 53, (a. 1852)

ACKNOWLEDGEMENTS AND BACKGROUND:

Ramona Barth (Alna, Maine) brought much of the basic program together in the early 1970's and ignited the streets of Miami, Florida by burning Bible quotes at the Democratic Convention of 1972. In 1974, Ramona brought "A Feminist Exercise in Exorcism" to the General Assembly of the Unitarian Universalist Association in New York City. The next year, exorcisms spread across the country; sexist quotes were burned from Boston to Berkeley.

KNOW, Inc. printed Ramona's program and I read it. But I did not decide to expand, revise and present the material before public audiences until Alyce Slabic (Stockton, California) mentioned that she would like to see an "Exorcism on Sexism" presented to the annual women's retreat sponsored by the Women and Religion Task Force, Pacific Central District, of the Unitarian Universalists.

Several women, calling ourselves "The Militant Menopausal Women," were already performing Marylou Hadditt's "Rights of Passage: A Celebration of Mid Life and Menopause" before groups such as O.W.L., N.O.W., and Bay Area Unitarian Universalist churches and fellowships — so we offered *Why We Burn: Sexism Exorcised*. Our performances were smash successes! After a Womyn's Week program at San Jose State University, we even made the headlines of *The Spartan Daily*: WOMEN BURN THE BIBLE! Many of the quotes were published in the Nov/Dec 1983 issue of *The Humanist* magazine.

Special thanks to Charlotte Suskind, Marjorie Hart, Jenny Grover Vickie Merryman, B.J. Bryan, Shirley Clyde, Joy Stinson, Rosemary and Howard Matson and all the other feminists who have burned sexist put-downs in our exorcisms.

My wish is for this program — this consciousness raiser — to be performed throughout the land. No, throughout the world!

— Meg Bowman, 1987

INSPIRATION

Though scripture oft inspires me
to reverence...or reverie,
at least; where woman and her lot,
her needs ignored, her name forgot
is subject matter, sacred page
inspires laughter, tears...or rage.

> — Ruth Van Gorder
> Lake Ariel, Penn.
> *Kyriokos*, 3/15/80

CREDITS AND DEDICATION

Thanks to three of the smartest women I know for editing and for suggestions: Barbara Glass, Trudy Kilian and Gina Allen.

Heartfelt thanks to our Sisters who gave permission to use their material: Ramona Barth, who started it all; Ruth Van Gorder, for inspiring us, and Jenny Grover, for writing "The New Battle Hymn of the Republic," which may very well become "our song" as we enter the second phase of the American Revolution.

Why We Burn: Sexism Exorcised is dedicated to all the other feisty feminists who, throughout the centuries, have "burned" in indignation; your anger is not forgotten.

> — Meg Bowman, 1987

TABLE OF CONTENTS

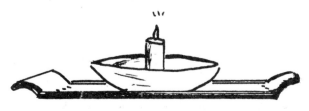

An Example of a Flyer:

THE FIRST UNITARIAN CHURCH OF SAN JOSE
INVITES YOU TO A MOST UNUSUAL PROGRAM

Sunday
January 16th
11:00 a.m.

WHY WE BURN:
SEXISM EXORCISED

"Good theater; good theology:
Don't miss it!"

Presented by:
Women & Religion Task Force
First Unitarian Church
160 N. Third Street
San Jose, CA
292-3858

Who was Anne Hutchinson?

One Hundred women are not worth a single testicle. — Confucius

"The Bible and the church have been the greatest stumbling blocks in the way of women's emancipation."

—Elizabeth Cady Stanton

"Men are superior to women." — The Koran

"I'll go forth, but I won't multiply!"

©1981, reprinted from *New Woman*
by permission of Artemis Cole.

-48-

WHY WE BURN: SEXISM EXORCISED

This is a "consciousness-raiser" which exposes in dramatic form the inherent sexism permeating major religions in the world. The highlight of this program is when a number of sexist quotes from some of the church fathers and philosophers are read, set on fire and burned.

The complete program is in eight parts and is about an hour long. Much of the material is optional and this program can be revised and shortened to about a twenty minute presentation.

Rehearsal: There is no need for the cast to memorize parts, but *there should be at least one rehearsal* for: (1) timing; (2) correct pronunciation of words such as Koran (core-ann); (3) inclusion of dates and saying "quote" and "unquote"; and (4) speaking loudly and clearly. The cast will also need to practice *looking at the person who is speaking* (and *not* down at the script).

Cast: The four to six readers can be all women, or women and one or two men.

Promotional Materials: Here are some examples of promotional materials which can be used to publicize this program:

Example No. 1: *Unitarian-Universalist Newsletter*

WHY WE BURN: SEXISM EXORCISED

Our Women and Religion Task Force *challenges* the sexism in all major religions. Come and watch us *burn* as we read the words of the church fathers and discover with us our patriarchal religious heritage — the church — the oldest and most entrenched *enemy* of women. (A most unusual consciousness raiser!)

Example No. 2: *Newsletter*

Tracing the "herstory" of patriarchal religions, we (or list names of participants) read the words of the church fathers and then exorcise the sexism out of religion. We (or they) challenge over

6,000 years of patriarchy. We (or they) challenge all major religion — all sexist and in need of purging. Come watch us (or them) burn and discover with us (or them) the words from our Judeo-Christian tradition. Come watch us (or them) smoke out the most entrenched enemies of women.

Example No. 3:

The Stockton, California Unitarian church (3/84) requested in their Newsletter that members and friends bring a sexist quote they would like to have exorcised: "Do you have a sexist quote you'd like to have exorcised? Bring it to church next Sunday for our SEXISM EXORCISED program."

At the end of the "Exorcism" (Part VI), invite your audience to bring forth their sexist quote, read it and then exorcise it by burning it.

Example No. 4:

On the walls where your program will be held, place pictures of Anne Hutchinson and Sonia Johnson and/or pictures of women in veils (shadors), posters of vaginal mutilations, witch burnings and other atrocities against women initiated by and/or supported by churchmen. Books by Sonia Johnson, Charlotte Perkins Gilman, and about Anne Hutchinson can be put on display.

"Feminism is changing the roots of the soul of the world."
                                                        -Sonia Johnson

An Example of A Complete Program

PARTS

Part I — **Song**: "Sisters, Sisters" on tape*/ or a Carolyn McDade or Holly Near song (optional).

PART II — **Feminist Prayer** (see p. 53), or the poem "Inspiration" by Ruth Van Gorder (see p. 46).

Part III — **Responsive Readings**: "Anne Hutchinson" (optional: see p. 55).

Part IV — **Essay**: Comparison of Anne Hutchinson and Sonia Johnson (optional: see pp. 57-58).

Part V — **Song**: "Excommunicate" on tape* (optional).

PART VI — **Program: Why We Burn: Sexism Exorcised**
> Section 1: Readings
> Section 2: Burnings
> Section 3: Readings

Part VII — **Song**: "The New Battle Hymn of the Republic" by Jenny Grover/ or "Song for Equal Suffrage" by Charlotte Perkins Gilman (1911)/ or "Battle Hymn of Women" (optional: see pp. 75-83).

Part VIII — **Closing**: Quote from Sonia Johnson's book, *From Housewife to Heretic* (optional: p. 85).

Create your own program, e.g. your program could consist of only Parts II and VI.

*This was available to us from:
Mormons for E.R.A.
Tape: "Sisters" by Cheryl Dalton
2055 Laurelwood Rd., Sp. 11
Santa Clara, CA 95054

Cost: $10.00 ppd.

PROPS:

1. *Table* placed in front of audience.
2. Metal *tray* (covered with aluminum foil).
3. *Bowl* (*not* plastic) which can be covered with aluminum foil.
4. Large *candle* placed in bowl (which sits on the tray).
5. Book of *matches* to light the large candle before the performance.
6. Four to six *small candle holders* with *candles* in them (use the same number of candles as number of readers).
7. (optional) Cassette player and cassette tape, "Sisters" by Cheryl Dalton (see p. 51).
8. Copies for the audience of the program, which may include the "Feminist Prayer" (see p. 53), and you may duplicate back-to-back on one sheet of paper the Responsive Reading and any song(s) and/or other material(s) you select for the program.
9. Rather than cut up this book, type or photocopy the quotes (Part VI, Section 2, pp. 64-69) and then cut out each quotation consecutively and divide them consecutively, into the number of readers so that each member of the cast has a stack of quotations to read. Use *paper clips* to keep these strips of paper together and place each stack on the table in front of where each reader will stand.
10. *A copy of Section 1 and Section 2 of Part VI* of the program for each reader.

OPTIONAL:

Tablecloth — bright red or whatever looks dramatic with the decor.

Flowers on the table, or in front of the table.

Books on display, perhaps sitting up on the table, e.g.:

From Housewife to Heretic, Sonia Johnson, Doubleday, 1981.

The Feminist Attack on the Bible, Elizabeth Cady Stanton, Arno Press (re-print 1974), original date 1895/1898.

When God Was A Woman, Merlin Stone, Harcourt Brace Javanovich, 1976.

Woe to the Women: The Bible Tells Me So, Annie Laurie Gaylor, Freedom From Religion Foundation, Box 750, Madison, WI 53701. (1981)

Herland (1915-1979) and *Charlotte Perkins Gilman Reader* (1980), Pantheon Books (she wrote the lyrics to "Song for Equal Suffrage").

Freedom Under Siege, Madalyn Murray O'Hair, Tarcher, 1974.

An Example of a Printed Program

WHY WE BURN: SEXISM EXORCISED

Prelude/Opening: "Sisters, Sisters" . . . . . Cheryl Dalton tape

Feminist Prayer . . . . Led by (Name)

FEMINIST PRAYER

Our Mother, who art in heaven
Sister shall be thy name
Our washin's done, Our kitchen's clean
On earth and it isn't heaven.
Give us this day equality
And forgive us our disparagements
As we forgive those who disparage against us.
And lead us not into Home Economics,
But deliver us into politics.
For *there* is the power
And the glory
And the money
Forever . . .

A-Woman

Welcome and Announcements . . . . (Name)

Offertory (if a church program) and Greeting

Responsive Reading: "Anne Hutchinson" and "Comparison of Anne Hutchinson and Sonia Johnson" . . . . (Name)

Music: "Excommunicate" . . . . Cheryl Dalton tape

Program: "Why We Burn: Sexism Exorcised"
. . . . (list cast, or use group name)

Song: "The New Battle Hymn of the Republic"
by Jenny Grover . . . . Led by (Name)

Closure: Reading from Sonia Johnson's book
From Housewife to Heretic . . . . (Name)

The suggested program takes about one hour to perform and is for a feminist audience. Feel free to shorten the format, to use less militant music, etc., as performing before a group of ardent feminists, such as an N.O.W. meeting or a Womyn's History Week program is different from performing before a mixed group of Humanists, Unitarians, etc. Omit singing a song when presented before a class.

"Feminism is the greatest spiritualist revolution in the history of the world.

-Sonia Johnson

"As long as god is male, males are gods."
-Mary Daly

PART III

ANNE HUTCHINSON
(1591-1643)

Anne Hutchinson arrived with her husband and family in the Massachusetts Bay Colony in 1634.

— WHO ARE YOU, ANNE HUTCHINSON?

I am the daughter of a minister. I am the mother of 15 children, a midwife and a healer.

— AND ARE YOU NOT A DEVIANT WOMAN?

Men gather after church to debate the sermon. I gather women at my home to do likewise.

— YOU LEAD WOMEN INTO SIN.

Wives often develop independent views from their husbands, and the established church.

— THE CHURCH IN THE MASSACHUSETTS BAY
COLONY BELIEVES THE HOLY SPIRIT COMES
ONLY TO THOSE SELECTED BY GRACE.

We women have developed a more generous viewpoint. We believe the holy spirit is in everyone.

— YOU WOMEN DARE TO OPENLY DISAGREE
WITH YOUR HUSBANDS —
AND THE CHURCH?

Occasionally, we even walk out of the church.

— ANNE HUTCHINSON, WE CHARGE YOU WITH
HERESY:
"BEING A HUSBAND RATHER THAN A WIFE,
A PREACHER RATHER THAN A HEARER,
AND A MAGISTRATE RATHER THAN A
SUBJECT."

I rely on my intelligence and my inner intuition: If this be sin, so be it.

— ANNE HUTCHINSON, YOU ARE EXCOMMUNI-
CATED AND BANNED FROM THE COLONY.

My defiant spirit lingers. Someday women will be church leaders and change the world.

—mb

Banished in 1638, thirty-five families followed Anne Hutchinson and her family to Rhode Island. In 1643 they went to the shores of Long Island Sound where Indians who had been defrauded of their land thought she was one of their enemies; she and most of her family were killed. Twenty years later, the one person who had spoken up for her during her long trials, Mary Dyer, was hanged by the Massachusetts Bay Government, along with two other Quakers, for "rebellion, sedition, and presumptuous obtruding themselves."

NOTE: Next door to 25 Beacon Street, Boston, Massachusetts, the continental office of Unitarian Universalists, are statues of two women: Anne Hutchinson and Mary Dyer.

Mary Dyer *(1618-1660). Quaker woman hanged on Boston Common when she returned to Massachusetts after banishment to aid persecuted Quakers.*
"I rather chuse to Dye than to live."

Anne Hutchinson *(1591-1643). Quaker theologian, midwife, and the mother of 15, banished from Massachusetts for her religious beliefs.*
"I desire to know wherefore I am banished."

PART IV

ANNE HUTCHINSON AND SONIA JOHNSON*:
A COMPARISON

ESSAY

In the year 1637, ANNE HUTCHINSON was excommunicated by the Massachusetts Bay Colony; 342 years later SONIA JOHNSON was excommunicated by the Mormons. That was in 1979.

What are some of the similarities — and the differences — between these two women and the times in which they lived?

First, some similarities: Both were threatened by the patriarchal authorities; both were challenged by the male clergy. *A* telling *B* what to do! If not, we will remove you!

Both women went on trial for heresy — a "false" religion — and the *Prosecutor*, and *Judge* and the *Jury* were one, the religious brethren.

In both cases, there were NO women on "the jury." Both were found guilty and both were excommunicated; it was the church's "right."

Both women loved their churches — religion was important to both of them. Sonia was the organist and a leader in her ward. Anne was *the* leader not only of the women, but also of many men.

Now, let's look at some of the differences:

ANNE HUTCHINSON had no place to appeal; SONIA JOHNSON did appeal and, of course, the United States Constitution guaranteed Sonia freedom of — and from — religion.

Anne was exiled; Sonia could not be exiled for she is a citizen of the United States.

Anne, who had followed John Cotton from England, held meetings in her house — for women and men. The clergy ordered her to cease and desist. Sonia, because of the separation of church and state, could peaceably assemble in her home.

Anne had only Mary Dyer in her support group; Sonia has thousands of women and men supporting her. Sonia also has access to the media, non-existent during Anne's long trials. And, Sonia has had her book *From Housewife to Heretic* published, and ran as presidential candidate for the Citizens Party in 1984.

Governor John Winthrop presided over Anne's trials — (and these were forerunners of the Salem Witch Trials) — and

*Pronounced SONE-YA.

Anne was suspected of being a witch. She was forced to stand during the arduous weeks of her last trial when she thought she was pregnant — again! When it was discovered that it was not a pregnancy, but fibrous tumors, it was considered proof of witchcraft.

Well, both women have gone down in history — strong, intelligent, revolutionary, radical, feisty, soft-spoken mavericks and wave-makers — who, because of the power of their convictions, initiated social change. They spoke out and acted on their convictions. They did not give up, even when threatened by the good brethren with *excommunication.*

(Optional) Please listen now to the song "Excommunicate," written and sung by Cheryl Dalton, a leader of Mormons for the E.R.A.*

*Cassette, *Sisters, Sisters* (see p. 51).

Sonia Johnson

PART VI

PROGRAM

A FEMINIST EXERCISE IN EXORCISM

Cast stands behind the table with the tray, bowl, candles and stacks of quotations. Each reader has a copy of Section 1 and Section 3 of PART VI: PROGRAM. Consecutively, each reads one paragraph; when not reading, cast looks at person who is speaking, *not* at the script.

Section 1

THE OPENING

Reader:

1. In 1971 the women's group of St. Clement's Episcopal Church, New York City, rewrote the liturgy from the Book of Common Prayer, read sexist statements from the Bible, brought them to the altar, set them on fire and presented them as a burnt offering.

2. In 1972, on Mother's Day, women of the state of Maine followed suit in two Unitarian-Universalist churches, at a N.O.W. meeting in Portland, and at a Feminist Party gathering in Brunswick.

3. The same year, at the Democratic National Convention, women repeated the ritual in the streets of Miami Beach. Our coast-to-coast "burnings" in 1975 were a prelude to feminist fireworks set off in 1976, our Bicentennial, to "Remember the ladies," as Abigail Adams asked John to do in 1776. — John forgot.

4. From Berkeley to Boston, Maine to Miami, we have burned. Omaha women drew the biggest audiences as they ignited the streets of Nebraska. And, yes, radical feminism has even "played in Peoria" — pyromaniacally.

5. Why burn? The answer is simple. Read the Bible — the Koran — the theologians and philosophers of the world. Look in your hymnals and then ask, "What better way to raise the religious consciousness of obtuse, callous, sexist societies?"

6. But not your church, you say?

7. Attend almost any Board meeting, Council or Membership meeting and close your eyes — : Most of the voices you hear will be male.

8. Not long ago, at a church meeting, a woman proposed a solution to a problem. She was ignored. She proposed it again . . . and later, again. Well into the meeting, the chair*man* suddenly came up with a solution to their problem — it was the same one the woman had proposed an hour ago. Coming from the mouth of the chair*man*, it now had credence. *Now* it was taken seriously.

9. Our foremothers, Susan B. Anthony, Elizabeth Cady Stanton, Matilda Joslyn Gage, Sojourner Truth and Alice Paul knew that the major force *against* women's rights came from the male clergy.

10. Elizabeth Cady Stanton said, (quote) "The Bible and the church have been the greatest stumbling blocks in the way of women's emancipation." (close quote). She got together with other women and they put together the "Women's Bible" — noting all passages that relate to women.

11. Betty Friedan told the world (including the Pope personally) (quote) "the church is the enemy."

12. In 1973, a Roman Catholic theologian told a convocation of Lutheran pastors in St. Paul, Minnesota that the Judeo-Christian tradition is (quote) " . . . the oldest and most entrenched enemy" of women striving for "full human dignity and personhood."

13. Dr. Rosemary Ruether, one of the first two women to become a lecturer at Harvard Divinity School, said that since the time of the earliest Christian fathers, women have been viewed as (quote) ". . . flesh, a sort of headless body." — "the symbol of sin" — for the spiritually superior male to control and use, "either as the means of procreation or the remedy for their sexual desires."

14. Both the early fathers and the medieval theologians agreed "that for any spiritual companionship another male is always more suitable."

15. "Not too surprising," Ruether went on — "the most concerted foes of the women's movement in the 19th century and down to our own times have been the Christian clergy, and it has been the Biblical, especially the Pauline, texts which have been used continually as the bludgeon to beat women back into their traditional place." (close quote)

16. That same year — 1973 — Dr. Mary Daly, professor of theology at Boston College, spoke before the Nobel Conference: (quote) "Compare the high status of women under the Celts with that of women under Christianity . . . a patriarchal religion which functions to maintain patriarchy. Male Deity, the incarnation of God, in a male Christ, feminization of evil, sexist scriptures, disregard of women's experience are means by which this is achieved. A sexist society spawns a sexist religion, which, in turn, produces a sexist society."

17. In her book *The Church and The Second Sex*, Dr. Mary Daly notes that (quote) ". . . a woman's asking for equality in the church would be comparable to a black person's demanding equality in the Ku Klux Klan."

18. Rosemary Matson and Lucile Schuck Longview attended the United Nation's International Women's Conference in Copenhagen in 1980 where they discovered that among the hundreds of workshops scheduled, none were on Women and Religion. So, they scheduled two *Women and Religion* workshops. Both were attended by about 200 women coming from numerous and varied religions — Islam, Hindu, even two nuns from the Vatican. The women at both workshops concluded that *women will never have equal rights — will never be liberated — until either the major religions are abolished or women assume leadership and drastically change them.*

19. (READ SLOWLY) You say we are too radical? Read your history. Read your bibles. Read the words of the church fathers and the philosophers. It's all there.

20. Their words have been used against us, and so today — we will burn them . . . for it is time to exorcise the sexism out of religion!

21. We bring you typical biblical, philosophical and theological quotes.

22. We bring you . . . SEXISM EXORCISED!!!

"Let women stay at home and hold their peace."
-Aeschylus,
Seven Against Thebes, 1. 201 (467 B.C.)

*"Let Mary be excluded from among us,
for she is a woman, and not worthy of Life."*

— Last line of the Secret gospel of Thomas:
Simon Peter to the disciples.

Section 2

THE EXORCISM

A) Preparation:

1. Photocopy, delete, or type a copy of the following quotations.

2. Consecutively cut out each quotation; consecutively place those you wish to use in a pile.*

3. Consecutively divide that stack of quotations into the number of readers, i.e. if there are five readers, there should be five piles of quotes, one pile for each reader.

4. Place a paper clip on each pile to hold them together.

5. Place each pile of these strips of paper (each containing a quotation) on the table in front of the reader *before* the performance so that they are handy and can be read in consecutive order.

B) Performance:

1. When reading the quotations, be sure readers include the dates.

2. Participants watch each reader while s/he reads, and can laugh, scoff and make negative gestures (such as the thumbs down gesture and shaking their heads). HAVE FUN WITH THIS PART OF THE PROGRAM.

3. After reading each quotation, the reader folds the strip of paper (thus making it easier to handle), sets it on fire from the large candle in the center of the bowl, and quickly places the burning strip of paper on the *tray* to burn.**

Caution: If readers place the burning paper *in* the bowl, the candle melts, causing a big fire in the bowl.

---

*Feel free to add and/or delete quotes.

**If you prefer *not* to burn the slips of paper, you may (a) place them in a vessel designated as woman's body noting these ideas have gone into her psyche, (b) shred them (as junk mail) into a wastebasket, or (c) place them in a toilet bowl and pretend to flush, using appropriate sound effects. These, of course, do not fit into the theme of WHY WE BURN.

THE EXORCISM

Type or photocopy the following quotations (add your own, if you wish) and place them, consecutively, into stacks for the readers. Use a paper clip to keep them together. (NOTE: Emphasis added by author.)

1. One of the worst sexists was the revered sage, CONFUCIUS. This respected religious leader said, "One hundred women are not worth a single testicle."

2. Confucius, respected authority on how to live, wrote in the *Confucian Marriage Manual* (551-479 B.C.E.): The five worst infirmities that affect the female are indocility, discontent, slander, jealousy and silliness . . . Such is the stupidity of women's character, that it is incumbent upon her, in every particular, to distrust herself and to OBEY HER HUSBAND.

3. ARISTOTLE, an important Greek philosopher who lived from 384-322 B.C.E. said: "The female is a female by virtue of a certain lack of qualities — a natural defectiveness."

4. ARISTOTLE also said, "A proper wife should be as obedient as a slave."

5. HIPPOCRATES, so-called father of modern medicine, believed with Aristotle that there were two kinds of reproductive seeds. The strong seeds were male and the weak seeds were female.

6. The *Hindu Code of Manu*, dated about 250 B.C.E., regulates social customs and lists detailed precepts for daily life, such as (quote): "In childhood a woman must be subject to her father; in youth to her husband; when her husband is dead, to her sons. A woman must NEVER be free of subjugation."

7. Also from this most impressive law book, the *Code of Manu*: "If a wife has no children after eight years of marriage, she shall be banished; if all of her children are dead, she can be dismissed after ten years; and, if she produces only girls she shall be repudiated after eleven years."

8. TERTULLIAN, the founder of Western theology, said in A.D. 22: "Woman is a temple built over a sewer, the gateway to the devil. Woman, you are the devil's doorway. You should ALWAYS go in mourning and in rags."

9. Here is another of the first Latin Christian writer's gems. TERTULLIAN wrote: "Do you know that each of your women is an Eve? The sentence of God — on this sex of yours — lives in this age; the guilt must necessarily live, too. You are the gate of Hell, you are the temptress of the forbidden tree; you are the first deserter of the divine law."

10. And the church father ST. CLEMENT OF ALEXANDRIA wrote in 96 A.D.: "Let us set our womenfold on the road to goodness by teaching them . . . to display . . . submissiveness, to observe silence. Every woman should be overwhelmed with shame at the thought that she IS a woman."

11. ST. JOHN CHRYSOSTOM (345?-407 A.D.), Patriarch of Constantinople: "Among all savage beasts none is found so harmful as woman."

12. ST. AMBROSE, author and composer of hymns, bishop of Milan (340?-397): "Adam was led to sin by Eve and Eve by Adam. It is just and right that woman accept as lord and master him whom she led to sin." (I SAY, "EVE WAS FRAMED!")

13. The "moral majority" has been around a long time. Listen to this early Christian, church father ST. AUGUSTINE (354-430 A.D.): "Any woman who acts in such a way that she cannot give birth to as many children as she is capable of, makes herself guilty of that many murders . . . "

14. COUNCIL OF MACON: In the year 584, in Lyons, France, forty-three Catholic bishops and twenty men representing other bishops, held a most serious debate: ARE WOMEN HUMAN? After many lengthy arguments, a vote was taken. The results were 32 yes, 31 no. Women were declared human by ONE VOTE! (PAUSE) I will *not* burn this one!

15. The *Koran*, the catechism, the holy book of Islam, (Circa A.D. 650): Men are superior to women.

16. Daily prayer of the ORTHODOX JEWISH MALE (still in use today): "Blessed art thou, O Lord our God and King of the Universe, that thou didst NOT create me a woman."

17. The Old Testament, BOOK OF DEUTERONOMY (22:20-21) notes that if a woman be found not to be a virgin ". . . then they shall bring the damsel to the door of her father's house and the men of the city shall stone her with stones that she die."

18. EXODUS (20:17 and 22:16-17) declares as law that if a man seduces a virgin who is not betrothed (thus damaging the father's property) — he (the rapist) shall marry her. (CAN YOU IMAGINE HAVING TO MARRY YOUR RAPIST?!) If the father doesn't wish this, the rapist (quote) ". . . shall pay money equivalent to the marriage/bride price for virgins."

19. JOB (25:4): "How can he be clean that is born of woman?"

20. LEVITICUS (12:1-2, 5): And the Lord spake unto Moses saying: speak unto the children of Israel, saying: if a woman be delivered, " . . . and bear a *man*-child then she shall be unclean for seven days . . . .But if she bear a *maid*-child, then she shall be unclean for *two* weeks . . . "

21. In 1847, a British obstetrician, Dr. Simpson, used chloroform as an anesthetic in delivering a baby. A scandal followed, and the holy men of the Church of England prohibited the use of anesthetic in childbirth, citing Genesis (3:16): "God said to woman Eve, I will greatly multiply thy sorrow and thy pain in childbearing. In *pain* thou shalt bring forth children . . . and thy desire shall be to thy husband and he shall *rule over thee*."

22. ECCLESIASTES (7:26-28): "I find a woman more bitter than death; she is a snare, her heart a net, her arms are chains. No wickedness comes anywhere near the wickedness of a woman. May a sinner's lot be hers."

23. NEW TESTAMENT: CORINTHIANS (11:7-9): Man is the image of God . . . whereas woman reflects the glory of man. For man did not originally spring from woman, but woman was made out of man; and man was not created for woman's sake, but woman for the sake of man.

24. TIMOTHY (2:9-12, 15): I desire that "women should adorn themselves modestly and sensibly . . . *not* with braided hair or gold or pearls or costly attire . . . Let a woman learn in silence with all submissiveness. I permit no woman to teach or have authority over men; she is to keep silent. Yet women will be saved through bearing children, if she continues in faith and love and holiness, *with modesty*."

25. Also from the NEW TESTAMENT: CORINTHIANS (14:33-36): It is shameful for a woman to speak in church. Wives should regard their husbands as they regard the Lord.

26. Again, CORINTHIANS, same passage: Women are not permitted to speak, but should be subordinate. If there is anything they desire to know, let them ask their husbands at home.

27. EPHESIANS (5:22-24): "Wives, submit yourselves unto your . . . husbands . . . for the husband is the head of the house."

28. The noted misogynist ST. PAUL told women: "You must lean and adapt yourselves to your husbands. The husband is the head of the wife."

29. The Coptic text of the GOSPEL OF THOMAS (these are the Gnostic texts discovered in 1945) translates: (114) Simon Peter said to them, "Let Mary leave us, for women are not worthy of life." Jesus said, "I myself shall lead her in order to make her male, so that she too may become a living spirit resembling you males. For every woman who will make herself male will enter the Kingdom of heaven."

30. Moving into the Middle Ages, ST. THOMAS AQUINAS, the well-known 13th century Italian theologian said: "Woman is defective and accidental . . . and misbegotten . . . a male gone awry . . . the result of some weakness in the (father's) generative power. She is by nature of lower capacity and quality than man."

31. The renowned Protestant clergyman, MARTIN LUTHER, said: "God created Adam lord of all living creatures, but Eve spoiled it all."

32. I want all of you women to pay particular attention to this one! MARTIN LUTHER (1483-1546): "Women should remain at home, *sit still*, keep house and bear and bring up children."

33. Again, the leader of the Reformation, MARTIN LUTHER: "If a woman grows weary and, at last, dies from childbearing, it matters not. Let her die from bearing; she is there to do it."*

34. JOHN KNOX, 16th century founder of Scottish Presbyterianism, declared: Woman in her greatest perfection was made to serve and obey man, *not* rule and command him.

35. SAMUEL BUTLER, the English poet who lived from 1612 to 1680 wrote: "The souls of women are so small that some believe they've none at all."

36. English poet ALEXANDER POPE (1688-1744): "Most women have no character at all."

37. French philosopher JEAN JACQUES ROUSSEAU (1712-1778): The whole education of women ought to be relative to men. To please them, to be useful to them . . . to make life sweet and agreeable to them . . . these are the duties of women at all times and what should be taught them from their infancy.

Die Ethnik Martin Luthers, Althaus, p. 100; or, this may have been said by Philip Melancthon, associate of Luther in the Reformation.

38. NAPOLEON BONAPARTE (1769-1821) said: "Nature intended women to be our slaves . . . they are our property..." (and later) " . . . Women are nothing but machines for producing children."

39. German philosopher NIETZSCHE (1844-1900) wrote in *Thus Spake Zarathustra*: "Man shall be trained for war and women for the recreation of the warrior. All else is folly." *And*: "Thou goest to a woman? Do not forget thy whip."

40. Swiss Protestant theologian KARL BARTH (1886-1968) said: "Woman is ontologically subordinate to man."

41. POPE PIUS XII said in 1941 (He reigned 1939-1958): "The pains that, since original sin, a mother has to suffer to give birth to her child only draw tighter the bonds that bind them; she loves it the more, the more pain it has cost her."

42. Dr. C.W. Shedd, Presbyterian minister in Houston, Texas since 1955 wrote this advice to his son in a book, *Letters on How to Treat a Woman*, published in 1968: "It seems to me that nearly every woman I know wants a man who knows how to love with authority."

Women are "simple souls who like simple things and one of the simplest is one of the simplest to give . . . Our family airedale will come clear across the yard for one pat on the head. The average wife is like that. She will come across town, across the house, across the room, across to your point of view, and across almost anything to give you her love IF you offer her yours with some honest approval."

The status of Western women has steadily declined since the advent of Christianity — and is still declining . . . The Semitic myth of male supremacy was first preached in Europe to a pagan people to whom it came as a radical and astonishing novelty.

—Elizabeth Gould Davis
The First Sex (1971)
Chapter 14

OPTIONAL ENDINGS:

1. When this program is given in a church, one of the readers can say: "But surely we don't have any sexism in the (Unitarian, Presbyterian, Congregational . . .) church." While this is being said, s/he walks to a chair, picks up a hymnal and reads a preselected hymn with gender exclusive language which has a piece of blank paper in it. After reading the sexist lyrics, the reader *pretends* to tear out the page, but is actually (sleight of hand) tearing the blank sheet of paper, crumples it, takes it to the candle, ignites it and lets it burn on the tray. This makes for a dramatic ending and gives time for the other readers to pick up *Section 3* of the program and prepare for additional reading.

2. Having asked your audience (in your Newsletter . . .) to bring sexist quotes to exorcise, invite them to now step forward, read their quotation, and then set it on fire, thus exorcising it.

Although every organized patriarchal religion works overtime to contribute its own brand of misogyny to the myth of woman-hate, woman-fear, and woman-evil, the Roman Catholic Church also carried the immense power of very directly affecting women's lives everywhere by its stands against birth control and abortion, and by its use of skillful and wealthy lobbies to prevent legislative change. It is an obscenity — an all-male hierarchy, celibate or not, that presumes to rule on the lives and bodies of millions of women.

—Robin Morgan
Sisterhood is Powerful (1970)

Section 3

THE CLOSING

Participants read paragraphs consecutively;
readers look at each person as s/he reads.

Reader:

1. And so we smoke out the sexists, for these are the words that have been with us for hundreds of years.

2. These are the words used against us. Today, we burn them to take away their symbolic power.

3. Today we have raised the important issue of sexism in churches; we have raised our consciousness' on the role religion has played in our history.

4. We're exorcising ourselves of the downgrading, repressive attitudes that have made women feel less than human.

5. It is good theater and good theology.

6. A feminist exercise in exorcism is long overdue.*

7. We burn to break the cultural clutch of over one-hundred generations. This is truly a "worship" service, for we pay "worth" to what is worthy. We spew out what is not.

8. For exorcism is a kind of prayer — to expel the demons in the patriarchal father — passed on to the sons — and to the daughters — and to our mates and kin . . . and to ourselves.

9. So also do we expel the demons of feminist rage. Ours is a primal scream of fury at being zapped. We realize we have been brain-washed and culturally conditioned and socialized with sexist values.

*Or, if men are in the cast: A feminist exercise in exorcism in which men and women take part is long overdue.

10. NO MORE! We hereby reject the rape of the centuries. We symbolically set fire — we burn — we renounce the patriarchy in order to kindle our quest for personhood. We kindle our crusading fervor comparable to Martin Luther himself to reshape our misogynous society.

11. Elemental fire can both inflame and purge. William Lloyd Garrison burned the Constitution. Pacifists burned their draft cards. Today, we feminists in the same spirit, burn the raw, sadistic, sexist words of church fathers and old philosophers.

12. The phallic imperialism of the past must be highlighted for what it is — for today's patriarchal put-downs come from the machos of yesterday.

13. And opposition to women's rights has always come from the churches.

14. And we still have modern Mary Magdalenes who are still, in spirit, washing Jesus' feet. Modern Marys are still picking up and washing their men-folk's dirty socks, if not their feet, and putting the toilet seats down after them.

15. The suffering saint — the masochist — the martyr — the "enduring" — lives on. For many women are still "most comfortable" in the Judeo-Christian tradition and the patriarchal power structure it has begat.

16. Our "Sexism Exorcised" program is to create in women the "divine discontent" lauded by Emerson.

17. We challenge ALL major religions — ALL patriarchal — ALL paternalistic — ALL sexist; some of the most powerful institutions created by *man*.

18. We challenge over 6,000 years of history and sacred customs; we challenge patriarchy, the oldest of injustices.

19. We challenge the most sexist institutions we have — for there are *fewer* women in positions of power — ministers, rabbis, boards of directors — in religion than in education, in law, in business, in government — or *any other* basic institution.

20. The Catholic church still does not accept female clergy and has very few altar girls. *Men* are on the Boards and in the pulpits; women do the fundraising dinners and organize the rummage sales and bazaars. And, let's face it, religious institutions simply could not survive without women doing the work.

21. In 1974, Reverend Ms. Carter, one of the eleven "irregularly" ordained to the Episcopal priesthood, was serving communion to a young macho priest at a Riverside, California church. Said "holy man" sipped the wine, drew his fingernails across her hand on the chalice, drawing blood, and told her, "I hope you burn in hell!"

22. The young priest's hatred and fears, to the point of drawing blood, may or may not be an omen of bloodshed ahead as the Women's Revolution becomes the nation's second Revolution. That depends — on how many men and women like him come kicking and screaming into the Twenty-first century.

23. It is time for us to develop a philosophy and value system and practices of equality, of love, of fairness for *all* humans, men *and* women . . . for *all* of us, you *and* me.

24. Friends, _____*, support the "second wave" of feminism! Let's build a world where the flame of equality burns bright. Let's exorcise sexism!

*Specify your audience, e.g. Congregationalists, Unitarians . . .

(All readers light a small candle from the large candle, hold the lit candle in front of them, and then say in unison*:)

WE BURN: WE PURGE SEXISM FROM PATRIARCHAL CHURCHES AND THEIR CHAUVINIST LEADERS.

WE BURN: WE INFLAME THE ANGER AND RAGE WITHIN US.

WE BURN: THE HATEFUL, SADISTIC, SEXIST WORDS OF THE CHURCH FATHERS.

WE BURN: FOR A WORLD OF PEACE AND EQUALITY AND LOVE.

WE BURN: SO THAT WE MAY ALL BE ON FIRE TO CREATE A BETTER WORLD.

*This may be used after PART VIII, **THE CLOSING,** to end the program.

PART VII

SONG

Select a song for the choir, a group, or the audience to sing; or, play a record or a tape; or, have one of the cast members play a guitar and sing a feminist song.

Examples:

1) Speaker: Will you please join us as (Name) leads us in singing a song written by Charlotte Perkins Gilman in 1911: "Song for Equal Suffrage."

2) Speaker: Let's now listen to Helen Reddy as she sings, "I am Woman"/ or Nina Simone singing, "I Wish I Knew How It Would Feel To Be Free."*

3) Speaker: Let's all sing "The New Battle Hymn of the Republic" by Jenny Grover. Copies are in your program. Let's hear it, nice and loud . . . Here we go!

*"I Am Woman," Helen Reddy, *Greatest Hits*, Capital #11367 and *I Am Woman*, #10699.

"I Wish I Knew How It Would Feel To Be Free," Nina Simone, *Nina Simone*, Victor (RCA) #1-4374.

THE NEW BATTLE HYMN OF THE REPUBLIC

by Jenny Grover
1984

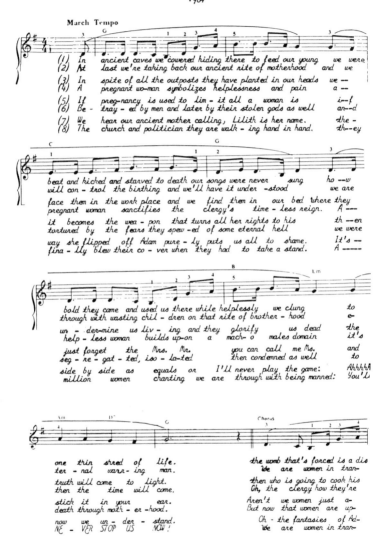

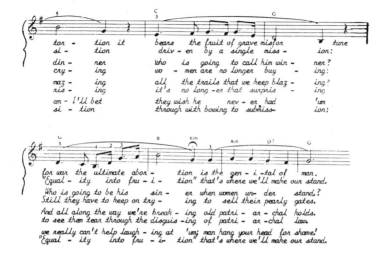

tor - tion it bears the fruit of grave misfor - tune
si - tion driv - en by a single miss - ion:

din - ner who is going to call him win - ner?
cry - ing wo - men are no longer buy - ing:

maz - ing all the trails that we keep blaz - ing?
ris - ing it's no long-er that surpris - ing

am - I'll bet they wish he nev - er had 'um
si - tion through with bowing to submiss- ion:

for war the ultimate abor - tion is the gen - i -tal of man.
"Equal - ity into fru - i - tion" that's where we'll make our stand.

Who is going to be his sin - er when women un - der stand.?
Still they have to keep on try - ing to sell their pearly gates.

And all along the way we're break - ing old patri - ar - chal holds.
to see them tear through the disguis -ing of patri - ar -chal law.

we really can't help laugh - ing at 'um; man hang your head for shame!
"Equal - ity into fru - i- tion" that's where we'll make our stand.

FEMINISM LIVES

The original sheet music cover for *Battle Hymn of the Republic*. Note that Julia Ward Howe is identified by her husband's name.

(Julia Ward Howe, Unitarian, founded Mother's Day. Originally set in June, it was a day to be set aside for peace.)

BATTLE HYMN OF WOMAN
(To the tune of "Battle Hymn of the Republic")

Mine eyes have seen the glory
of the flames of women's rage,
Smouldering for centuries
now burning in this age.
We no longer will be prisoners
in the same old gilded cage.
That's why we're marching on.

CHORUS

You have told us to speak softly
to be gentle and to smile,
Expected us to change ourselves
with every passing style.
Said the only work for women
was to clean and type and file.
That's why we're marching on.

CHORUS

It's we who've done your cooking,
done your cleaning, kept your rules.
We gave birth to all your children
and we taught them in your schools.
We've kept this system running,
but we're laying down our tools.
For we are marching on.

CHORUS

You think that you can buy us off
with golden wedding rings.
You never pay us half the profit
that our labor brings.
Our anger eats into us
we'll no longer bow to kings.
That's why we're marching on.

CHORUS

CHORUS:
Move on over or we'll move on over you
Move on over or we'll move on over you
Move on over or we'll move on over you,
For women's time has come.

SONG FOR EQUAL SUFFRAGE

Lyrics by Charlotte Perkins Gilman, 1911
(To the tune of "Battle Hymn of the Republic")

1. DAY OF HOPE AND DAY OF GLORY AFTER
     SLAVERY AND WOE,
   COMES THE DAWN OF WOMEN'S FREEDOM,
     AND THE LIGHT SHALL GROW AND GROW
   UNTIL EVERY MAN AND WOMAN EQUAL
     LIBERTY SHALL KNOW,
   IN FREEDOM MARCHING ON

        GLORY GLORY HALLELUJAH
        GLORY GLORY HALLELUJAH
        GLORY GLORY HALLELUJAH
        IN FREEDOM MARCHING ON.

2. NOT FOR SELF BUT LARGER SERVICE, HAS OUR
     CRY FOR FREEDOM GROWN:
   THERE IS CRIME, DISEASE AND WARFARE IN
     A WORLD OF MEN ALONE,
   IN THE NAME OF LOVE WE'RE RISING NOW
     TO SERVE AND SAVE OUR OWN,
   AS PEACE COMES MARCHING ON

        GLORY GLORY HALLELUJAH
        GLORY GLORY HALLELUJAH
        GLORY GLORY HALLELUJAH
        AS PEACE COMES MARCHING ON.

3. WE WILL HELP TO MAKE A PRUNING HOOK
     OF EVERY OUTGROWN SWORD
   WE WILL HELP TO KNIT THE NATIONS
     IN CONTINUING ACCORD
   IN HUMANITY MADE PERFECT IS
     THE GLORY AND REWARD
   AND OUR WORLD IS MARCHING ON

        (CHORUS)

-81-

OUR TRUTH WILL NOW RING OUT!
(To the tune of "Battle Hymn of the Republic")

Say, sisters, won't you join us
    as we try to change the world?
Oh, the banner of Equality
    our movement has unfurled.
We've taken off our aprons
    and the challenge has been hurled -
Our Truth Will Now Ring Out!

(Chorus)

Glory, glory, halelujah,
Glory, glory, halelujah,
Glory, glory, halelujah,
Out Truth Will Now Ring Out!

Say, brothers, won't you join us
    in our struggle to be free,
We can make this earth a better place
    for you as well as me,
We'll put the past behind us,
    and new vistas we will see -
Our Truth Will Now Ring Out!

(Chorus)

Oh, my sisters and my brothers,
    what a world we'll live in then,
We will learn about each other,
    and we'll call each other friend,
We'll journey on together
    towards a future without end -
Our Truth Will Now Ring Out!

(Chorus)

— Words by Vicki Siska Wilson

FEMINIST BLUES
(Tune: "The Battle Hymn of the Republic")

The time has come, dear sisters, to begin the fight anew
We didn't get the ERA by June '82
We won't give up the struggle; there is so much left to do
That's why we're marching on

(Chorus)

To the women in the kitchens, in the factories, on the farms
In offices, in classrooms, let this be a call to arms
From coast to coast keep singing out and sounding the alarm
Now we are marching on

(Chorus)

In the names of those who went before we struggle on today
We can't give up; we won't give up; we're in this fight to stay
The sun will rise on freedom yet; oh, we will have our day
If we keep marching on

(Chorus)

In the spirit of Elizabeth and good old Susan B.
We'll rally 'round the flag again for all the world to see
The fight will not be over until women all are free
That's why we're marching on

(Chorus)

Thru the words of Sonia Johnson our confidence is steeled
Her courage will inspire us, for she will never yield
With justice as our sword, the love of womankind our shield
Now we are marching on

(Chorus)

Move on over or we'll move on over you
Move on over or we'll move on over you
Move on over or we'll move on over you
For women's time has come.
                                        -Verses by Harriette Ramos

GLORY, GLORY, LESBIAN NATION
(To the tune of "Battle Hymn of the Republic")

Mine eyes have seen the glory
   of the coming of the day
When all Lesbians are united
   and we turn the whole world gay.
And when we have converted them,
   converted they shall stay —
Our truth is marching on!

(Chorus)

Glory, glory, Lesbian Nation,
Glory, glory, Lesbian Nation,
Glory, glory, Lesbian Nation,
Our truth is marching on!

We shall find them in the suburbs
   and the Catholic boarding schools,
We shall find them in the cities
   and the office typing pools,
We shall try to find them young,
   before they've turned them into fools —
Our truth is marching on!

(Chorus)

We shall lure them from their husbands,
   and establishment careers,
We shall open up their closet doors,
   and overcome their fears,
We shall demonstrate the pride
   of being unrepentant queers —
Our truth is marching on!

(Chorus)

— From *Lesbian Voices*
Rosalie Nichols, editor
Summer 1976

-84-

PART VIII

CLOSING

To close our program, I wish to read the last paragraph of Sonia Johnson's book *From Housewife to Heretic.*

In her book *From Housewife to Heretic*, Sonia Johnson pleads with us, "Please do not give up now." Sonia quotes Susan B. Anthony speaking to a group of young women, and feeling frustrated that after spending 70 years working for women's rights — she could not get some women to care enough to spend seventy seconds, (quote) "I really believe I shall explode if some of you young women don't wake up and raise your voices in protest. I wonder if when I'm under the sod — or cremated and floating in the air — I shall have to stir you and others up. How can you *not be all on fire*?" (close quote)

Sonia closes her book (quote): "And so I pray, 'Susan (B. Anthony), Elizabeth (Cady Stanton), Sojourner (Truth), Alice (Paul) — all of you great liberty-loving women whose atoms float over our land — come back to us now and stir us up. Right now, when there is still time to win the struggle you so courageously began. Come back and ignite us again. MAKE US BURN AS YOU BURNED. Dear Sisters (and Brothers), help us be all on fire!' "*

---

*Johnson, Sonia, *From House-Wife to Heretic,* (Doubleday), 1981, p. 406 (emphasis added).

She was trying to get rid of a religious hangover.

> — Simone de Beauvoir
> *Memoirs of a Dutiful Daughter* Part IV

———

I look forward with great anticipation to the death of the Church. The sooner it dies, the sooner we can be about the business of living the gospel.

> — Sally Gearhart
> *The Lesbian and God-The-Father, or All the Church Needs Is A Good Lay — On Its Side*, (1972)

———

In the Judeo-Christian creed the male body is the temple of God, while the female body is an object made for man's exploitation.

> — Elizabeth Gould Davis
> *The First Sex*, (1971)
> Chapter 9

———

Clergy are father figures to many women, and sometimes they are threatened by another woman accomplishing what they see as strictly male gods. But I can see them replacing that feeling with a sense of pride that women can have that role.

> — Sally Priesand
> Quoted in *Women at Work*
> by Betty Medsger (1975)

DOUBLE-CROSSED

BY THE

DOUBLE STANDARD

By

MEG BOWMAN

A program in six parts
for a cast of from two to eight
women and one or two men.

Entire program: 45 to 60 minutes
Skit only: 15 to 20 minutes

Roman Law: "If thou dost take thy wife in adultry," says Cato, "thou mayest kill her without trial and with impunity; but, if thou dost commit adultry thyself, she shall not and dare not so much as lay a finger on thee."

-George Thomson
Studies in Ancient Greek Society
(NY: International Pub., 1949), p. 93
Citing Aulus Gellius, 10, 23.

Acknowledgements

Thanks to Pat Stanton (wherever you are!) for the ideas in the satirical skit, *The Boss*, and warm fuzzies to Trudy Kilian for editing.

mb

INTRODUCTION

DOUBLE-CROSSED BY THE DOUBLE STANDARD is a delightful and educational program which can be used for programs, such as during Women's History Week, and in college classrooms. It traces the origin and development of the double standard as it relates to men and women, and then concentrates on the status of women in the United States today. It is a "consciousness raiser" which need not be rehearsed as long as someone is responsible for the props and someone directs the action.

No memorizing is necessary. One rehearsal is suggested, but not necessary, before presenting the reading to an audience. A rehearsal helps the cast learn where to sit/stand, how the parts of the program follow one another, how to pronounce certain words, and gives the cast an opportunity to practice timing (which is important in the skit, *THE BOSS*).

There are six parts to this program, plus two visualizations on sex role reversal and three lyrics to songs. Feel free to add materials or to delete any parts. If your time is limited, parts of the program, such as the skit *THE BOSS* (Part IV), which takes about 15 minutes to perform, can be used alone.

The cast may vary from three to ten persons and be all women or include one or two men. I usually use five women and one or two men in my productions.

— Meg Bowman
1987

> Women are not altogether in the wrong when they refuse the rules of life prescribed in the world. foresomuch as men have established them without their consent.
>
> -Montaigne (1595)

At age 50, Barbara Walters was the grande dame of television and Brinkley was the brash kid taking Walter Cronkite's place.
-Ron Owens, KGO Radio
5/13/86

Women are allowed to stay on TV as long as they don't *look* old.

PREFACE

I first became aware of the double standard during the 1940s. We lived in a small town in North Dakota and I wanted to learn to shoot pool, but girls weren't allowed in the pool room.

Winters are cold in North Dakota and skirts were short in the 1940s, but girls weren't allowed to wear slacks in school. In the summer, we girls learned to wear shorts under our skirts in order to play on the jungle gym and swings.

As a teacher, I couldn't wear slacks in the classroom until the 1970's. In the '60s, a woman was not permitted to sit on a bar stool in the state of Washington. Even in California, a wife could not go into business or buy a piece of property without her husband's written permission. Women were excluded from sitting on juries in South Carolina; and in Minnesota a husband could sue for divorce on the grounds of adultery, but a wife could not.

I remember touring Morocco in 1977 and having a drink in a bar with the manager of a small business. There was only one other woman in the bar, an employee — for Moroccan women who enter bars are considered "fallen" women. In many parts of the world, "respectable" women do not go to bars, or even public restaurants as these public domains are for men only; women stay home with the children.

This young man (in his 30s) told me he was saving money in order to marry. I asked him, "What would happen if your fiance saw you in here talking with me?" He sternly replied, "Why, nothing. She has nothing to say." I continued, "What would happen if you saw her talking to another man?" His body stiffened as he exclaimed, "I would never speak to her again! No! And I would not marry her!"

Later, after telling me how intelligent, how beautiful, how charming I was, his exact words were: "I would like to have coitus with you." This was "a line" I had never heard before and I burst out laughing! (and declined.)

The double standard is alive and well. The double standard is woven into the very fabric of societies all over the world. From the moment of birth when someone exclaims, "It's a boy!" or "It's a girl," expectations differ and sex role conditioning begins.

One study recorded people's statements when shown a baby wrapped in a blue blanket and identified as "Baby Boy Smith": "Wow, that's a big baby!" "Look at the size of those hands." "Kid sure has some broad shoulders." "Yeah, he'll be a football player for sure!" Later, the same baby, now wrapped in a pink blanket and identified as "Baby Girl Jones," elicited responses of: "Isn't she darling?" "So dainty. Look at those tiny hands." "I think she has dimples!" "A real cutie: She'll break some man's heart someday."

Historically, the double standard has often meant death to females. Infanticide has been a common method of population control, and it was female babies who were left out on rocks to die, or thrown into a river, or who had their brains smashed on rocks. For centuries, people who lived on Chinese sampans (boat people) tied ropes around boy toddlers. When a boy baby fell into the river, he was rescued. Girl babies seldom, if ever, had ropes tied around their waists. When a girl baby fell into the river, it was good riddance.

Double Crossed by the Double Standard relates primarily to the United States. It is educational, for it traces the origin and development of the double standard. This dramatic reading is also a "consciousness raiser" and an excellent introduction to a discussion on the double standard. I have used *Double Crossed by the Double Standard* in sociology classes and before public audiences, such as a Womyn's Film Festival, a Women's History Week program, at women's retreats and for N.O.W. meetings. If your time is limited, the satirical skit *The Boss* can be used alone.

Meg Bowman
San Jose, CA
1987

Man's love is of man's life a thing apart,
'Tis woman's whole existence.

— Lord Byron
Don Juan, Canto i, at 194 (1818)

TABLE OF CONTENTS

EGYPT: DOUBLE STANDARD

Egypt is more "modern" than most Islamic countries; here are some Egyptian laws:

Any Egyptian married woman who wishes to work outside the home needs her husband's authorization.

In 1984, a 17-year-old Egyptian girl was selected to be in the Olympics. Because she couldn't locate her father to get his written permission to leave the country, she was unable to compete.

Marriage between a Moslem woman and a non-Moslem man is forbidden, but a Moslem man can marry a Christian or a Jewish woman.

Under Moslem law, a man can have up to four wives (actually, he can have eight).

If a wife leaves her husband (even for reasons of battery), he has the legal right to obtain a court decision to force his wife's return.

If a woman tolerates battery or adultery by her husband early in their marriage without seeking an immediate divorce, she cannot obtain it later.

A man is allowed unilateral divorce and has a right to three divorces. A man has absolute right to divorce at any time; the wife has no such right.

Egyptian law states that a man who is "caught with a prostitute" is not imprisoned; instead, his testimony is used to convict and imprison the prostitute.

A wife is required by law to obey her husband.

In 1985 Egyptian women lost most of their civil rights.

An Example of a Program:

DOUBLE-CROSSED
BY THE DOUBLE STANDARD

An Historical Perspective
with a
Satirical Skit

Presented by _____

WELCOME........................ _____

COMMERCIAL: "Swandötter's Hungry
Woman Dinners" .... _____

Part I: *Dialogue*: "How To Tell a Businessman
from a Businesswoman," Dialogue 1 .... _____
                      (two readers) ...... _____

Part II: *Reading*: "A Herstory of the
Double Standard"..................... _____
                      (five readers) ...... _____
                      .... _____
                      .... _____
                      .... _____

Part III: *Dialogue*: "How To Tell a Businessman
from a Businesswoman," Dialogue 2 .... _____
                      (two readers) ...... _____

Part IV: Skit: *THE BOSS*..... Marge: _____
                             Joyce: _____
                         Waiter: _____

Part V: *Reading*: "The Summing Up" . . . . Readers

Part VI: *Dialogue*: "How To Tell a Businessman from a Businesswoman," Dialogue 3 . . . . _____
(two readers) . . . . . . _____

Part VII: *Visualization and Discussion*,
led by . . . . _____

Part VIII: *Closing Song*: "We Might Come In A Fighting," by Carolyn McDade, led by . . _____

Thank you for sharing this experience with us.

> *It occurred to me when I was 13 and wearing white gloves and Mary Janes and going to dancing school, that no one should have to dance backwards all their lives.*
> -Jill Ruckelshaus

ANOTHER EXAMPLE OF A PROGRAM

PROGRAM

DOUBLE-CROSSED
BY THE DOUBLE STANDARD

(full cast of ten people)

Introduction.........................(Reader #1)

Part I: "How To Tell a Businessman from a Businesswoman," Dialogue 1 ....(Readers #6 & 7)
(Dialogue between one woman and one man)

Part II: *A Herstory of the Double Standard* ..(Readers #1, 2, 3, 4 & 5)
(Reading by five women)

Part III: "How To Tell a Businessman from a Businesswoman," Dialogue 2........(Readers #6 & 7)
(Dialogue between same woman and man as in Part I)

Part IV: Introduction to skit.............(Reader #1)
THE BOSS ....(Readers #8, 9 & 10)
(Skit with two women and one man)

Part V: *The Summing Up*.....(Readers #1, 2, 3, 4 & 5)
(Reading by same five women as Part II)

Part VI: "How To Tell a Businessman from a Businesswoman," Dialogue 3 ....(Readers #6 & 7)
(Dialogue between same woman and man as in Parts I and III)

Part VII: *An Experience in Awareness* ....(Reader #1)
(Optional visualization)

Discussion, led by .... _____

CAST

The cast may vary from three to ten people.*

I. **Minimum cast of three:** Two women and one man (or a female dressed as a male).

II. **Maximum cast of ten:** Eight women and two men.

III. **Cast of six:** Four to five females and one or two males.

* * * * * * * * *

I. **Minimum cast of three:**

Two women and one man; *or* three women, with one dressed as a male.

Two women and one man.
1. Male reader has two roles: He reads the part of the BUSINESSMAN in the *Dialogues* (Part I, II, III, and IV — "How To Tell a Businessman from a Businesswoman") and plays the role of the WAITER (no dialogue) in the skit, *THE BOSS,* Part IV.

2. Two women real all other roles.

Part I: One woman and one man read "How To Tell a Businessman from a Businesswoman," **Dialogue 1.**

Part II: All three persons read "A Herstory of the Double Standard."

Part III: One woman and one man read "How To Tell a Businessman from a Businesswoman," **Dialogue 2.**

Part IV: Introduction to Skit: One reader.

                        Skit: All three readers.

Part V: All three persons read "The Summing Up."

Part VI: One woman and one man read "How To Tell a Businessman from a Businesswoman," **Dialogue 3.**

II Cast of six:

Five women and one man.

All six are readers. One woman and the male reader read Parts I,
III and VI, "How To Tell a Businessman from a Businesswoman,"
and two women and the man in the cast play the roles in the
satirical skit, "The Boss."

1. Male reader has two roles (see above).

2. The five women read the *Readings* (Parts II and V). One
   of the women reads the sharp dialogue of the
   BUSINESSWOMAN in Parts I, III, and VI. For the
   satirical skit *THE BOSS* (Part IV), two of the women
   readers move to the table to play the roles of MARGE
   and JOYCE.

III. Maximum cast of ten*:

Eight women and two men.

1. Two males: One for the part of the BUSINESSMAN in
   the *Dialogues* (Parts I, III, VI), and one to play the role
   of the WAITER in *THE BOSS* (Part IV).

2. Eight females: One for the part of the BUSINESSWO-
   MAN in the *Dialogues* (Parts I, III, VI), two to read the
   roles of MARGE and JOYCE in *THE BOSS* (Part IV),
   and five readers for the *Readings* (Parts II and V).

5 Readers for "A Herstory of the Double-Standard" and "The
Summing Up": reader #1: An older woman who ties the program
together. Readers #2, 3, 4 & 5: Women of any age.

2 Readers for "How To Tell a Businessman from a Businesswoman": Reader #6: Female dressed in a business suit. Reader
#7: Male dressed in a business suit.

3 Readers for the Skit, "The Boss": Readers #8 & 9 (MARGE &
JOYCE): Women in business attire. Reader #10 (WAITER): Man
(can be same person as Reader #7, as one person can play both
roles).

*NOTE: Program directions in this book are for a full cast of ten.

PROPS

1 table (such as a card table) with two chairs
1 tablecloth, white or red checkered
1 whiskey sour glass
2 martini glasses
  chairs for number of readers

Optional:

1 tray for waiter
1 pad and pencil for waiter to take the order
1 white towel for waiter to fold over his arm

The tablecloth, the whiskey sour glass and the martini glass are on the table. The other martini glass is "off-stage" where the waiter stands when not waiting on the table.

STAGE ARRANGEMENT

Full cast of ten:

**Dialogue Readers for
"How To Tell a Businessman
from a Businesswoman,"
Parts I, II, and VI.
Readers #7 & 6**

**Readers for "A Herstory of
the Double Standard" and
"The Summing Up,"
Parts II and V.
Readers #1 - 5**

**JOYCE & MARGE,
Skit, "The Boss,"
Part IV.
Readers #9 & 8**

**WAITER, Skit,
"The Boss,"
Part IV.
Reader #10**

TABLE

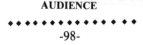

Cast of three:

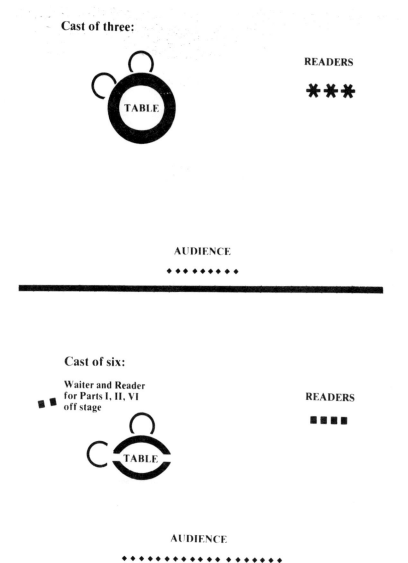

READERS

✳ ✳ ✳

TABLE

AUDIENCE

◆ ◆ ◆ ◆ ◆ ◆ ◆ ◆ ◆

Cast of six:

Waiter and Reader
for Parts I, II, VI
off stage

READERS

■ ■ ■ ■

TABLE

AUDIENCE

◆ ◆ ◆ ◆ ◆ ◆ ◆ ◆ ◆ ◆ ◆ ◆ ◆ ◆ ◆ ◆

NOTE: In this book, stage directions will be given for a full cast of ten.

PROGRAM PARTS

DOUBLE-CROSSED BY THE DOUBLE STANDARD

Part I   *How To Tell a Businessman from a
            Businesswoman,*
            One woman and one man. (Readers #6 & 7)

Part II   *A Herstory of the Double Standard*
            Five women. (Readers #1, 2, 3, 4 & 5)

Part III   *How To Tell A Businessman from a
            Businesswoman,* Dialogue 2
            (Readers #6 & 7)

Part IV   *THE BOSS* (a skit)
            Two women and one man. (Readers #8, 9 & 10)

Part V   *The Summing Up*
            Same five women as in Part II.

Part VI   *How To Tell a Businessman from a
            Businesswoman,* Dialogue 3
            (Readers #6 & 7)

Part VII   (Optional) *An Experience in Awareness*
            (Reader #1)

            Audience or classroom discussion
            after performance.

"COMMERCIAL"
(Optional)

SWANDÖTTER'S HUNGRY WOMAN DINNERS

For fun, you may wish to start your program with Reader #1 announcing:

Reader #1: Welcome to our program, ***Double Crossed by the Double Standard.***

But first, ladies and gentlemen, a commercial brought to you by Swandötter's Hungry Woman Dinners.

One of the readers can carry a sign across the stage which reads in large letters:

Male: Men, do you have a hungry woman at home?
Is your wife a big woman who has a hearty appetite?
Well, little man, buy Swandötter's "HUNGRY WOMAN DINNERS."
There's lots of food — double helpings — in "Hungry Woman Dinners."
Please your wife.
Satisfy your wife.
Get Swandötter's "Hungry Woman Dinners" — TODAY!

Reader #1: Thank you.

The first part of our program is called *How To Tell a Businessman from a Businesswoman.*

PART I

DIALOGUE:

HOW TO TELL A BUSINESSMAN
FROM A BUSINESSWOMAN
Dialogue 1

(for two readers)

Introduction:

READER #1:   Welcome to our program, *Double-Crossed by the Double Standard.*

It is being brought to you by the _____.

This first part is called *How To Tell a Businessman from a Businesswoman.*

READERS #6 & 7 *(a woman and a man dressed in business suits) face the audience center stage and in a sharp, biting repartee point to one another and exaggerate the dialogue.*

BUSINESSMAN: How To Tell A Businessman From a Businesswoman.

BUSINESSWOMAN points to BUSINESS-MAN and says:	BUSINESSMAN points to BUSINESSWOMAN and says:
A businessman is aggressive ...	A businesswoman is pushy.
He loses his temper because he's so involved in his job ...	She's just bitchy.
He's depressed from work pressures	She has menstrual tension.
He follows through	She doesn't know when to quit!
He's firm	She's stubborn.
He makes wise judgments.	She reveals her prejudices.
He is a man of the world	She's been around.
He isn't afraid to say what he thinks...............	She's opinionated.
He exercises authority	She's bossy; a real tyrant!
He's confident	She's conceited.
He stands firm	She's impossible to deal with.
He drinks because of excessive work pressure	She's a lush!

READERS #6 & 7 *sit down.* READER #1 *returns to center stage.*

PART II

READING:

A HERSTORY OF THE DOUBLE STANDARD

(for five readers)

Cast enters and sits down*, except for READER #1, *who stands center stage.*

READER #1:   **A Herstory of the Double Standard:**   *The double standard:*   A set of rules, behaviors, rights and values considered right and proper for some people, but not for others. A set of rules, behaviors, rights and values that are okay for one group of people, but not for another group.

Today (tonight), we explore the double standard as it relates to men and women.

The other four readers of "A Herstory of the Double Standard" stand center stage in a semi-circle so that as each paragraph is read, the readers look at the person reading (not at the script), and each should read slowly and clearly.

All Part II READERS *say in unison:*

ALL READERS:
WHAT'S GOOD FOR THE GOOSE IS GOOD FOR THE GANDER.
WHAT'S GOOD FOR THE GANDER IS GOOD FOR THE GOOSE.

Cast can shake their index fingers toward the audience on the last four words.

---

*If you wish, Parts II and V can be a "discussion" between two women.

1. The double standard is alive and well.

2. Until a few years ago, grounds for divorce in Minnesota included adultery; that is, a husband could sue for divorce on the grounds of adultery, but a wife could not.

3. Until 1975, the husband in California had the exclusive right to manage and control community property. Yes, he could sell the house and furniture, gamble away the family car, stocks, bonds and savings, and the wife was powerless to do anything about it.

4. Until July 1, 1975, a married woman in California could not own property or go into business without her husband's permission.

5. Women throughout Africa, Asia, and the Middle East are severely hampered by the double standard.

6. In 1979, the Ayatollah Khomeini (EYE-AH-TOLL-AH KOE-MEAN-EE), religious and political leader of Iran, dismissed women judges, banned female radio singers, and ordered women to wear the *chador* (veils instead of Western dress). When interviewed by an Italian journalist as to why an 18-year-old girl was executed for adultery while her lover was only beaten, the Ayatollah said, "Stop talking about these things. I am getting tired. These are not important matters."

7. An Egyptian woman still needs written permission from her husband to leave the country.

8. And she must have her husband's authorization to work outside the home.

9. How did it all begin?

10. Probably some 10 to 12 thousand years ago when agriculture and the domestication of animals evolved.

11. We can only theorize; no one was there to write it down. Humans did not learn to write until about 6 thousand years ago — and even if it had been recorded, time and the male perspective would have slanted the data.

12. We are going to explore *one* theory on how the double standard *may* have emerged.

13. Undoubtedly biology played a part in the development of sex roles: Men's work and women's work.

14. Many men, with broader shoulders (good for spear throwing) and narrower hips (good for running), became involved in hunting.

15. Many women, with broader hips and often pregnant or nursing, stayed near the rock ledge, the cave, the lake or the river — where they gathered roots and berries and gradually developed agriculture.

16. Men, accustomed to being with animals (and stronger), became the herders and began to designate areas of grazing land and, later, farmland, as belonging to them. As herders, they declared that the domesticated animals belonged to them.

17. Patriarchy began when men established private property — *my* camels, *my* goats, *my* land, *my* water well, *my* house. And soon thereafter, *my* wives, *my* children, *my* concubines, *my* servants, *my* slaves. *Mine!*

18. The emergence of patriarchy — male rule. And we've been in trouble ever since!

19. Now owning land and animals, the patriarch needed legal sons to inherit the camels, goats, sheep, land...

20. Because motherhood is a matter of fact and fatherhood is a matter of conjecture, how was the patriarch to know for sure that it was *his* seed that impregnated *his* "legal" wives?

21. A popular belief was that each seed — each sperm — was a complete human child which males deposited in a female for incubation purposes.

22. In order to ensure "legal" heirs (sons, that is) to inherit *his* land, *his* camels, *his* goats, *his* slaves, *his* name, *his* title . . . the patriarch segregated *his* wives to the women's quarters, put them in veils and provided eunuchs (U-NICKS) as guards.

23. Legal heirs (sons, that is) to inherit the property was the game plan. He begat — she did not bear. Remember the Biblical stories? Abraham begat Isaac, Isaac begat Jacob...? Women did not bear, men begat. Ancestry was traced on the male side only — lineage was patrilinear.

24. Women were relegated to the house, to the women's quarters; and they could not leave their prison without permission, without a chaperone.

25. Under Roman law, the patriarch decided which infants lived or died; he arranged all marriages, and he was entitled to sell his daughters as slaves — or even kill them.

26. The patriarch divided women into two types: The "Madonna" — the all-knowing, all-wise mother, and the "fallen woman." The Madonna was for marriage and bearing legal sons, and the "fallen woman" was for fun.

27. The patriarch and *his* sons — with the power — were free to roam. They often went to town to "dally-with-Delilah," the fallen woman. And when Delilah became pregnant, the partriarch declared that her "illegal" child could not lay claim to *his* property — to *his* name — or *his* throne.

28. Who else would have originated the crazy idea of an "illegitimate" child? A bastard? Certainly *no mother* would stigmatize her baby for life for being born "out-of-wedlock."

29. The patriarchs developed their "old boys network": *They* made the rules and the laws. *They* controlled the money. *They* had the power and women had, in effect, little — if any — social, legal or political status of their own.

30. The origin of the word "family" is the Latin "familia"* — meaning a man's slaves. His family was his wife, his children, his slaves.

31. Women of all classes were subordinate to men by law and by religion and by custom.

32. Marriages were arranged for economic and political purposes. *Daughters* were pawns to marry off — to merge families — to keep control of land, slaves, and serfs. *Wives* were to bear legitimate heirs to inherit the castle, the estate, the family name.

33. A wife who did not bear sons was replaced. The Shah of Iran got rid of two wives who bore only daughters. Henry VIII went through seven wives trying to sire a son.

34. Upper-class women were often socialized to be silly, childlike playthings — Barby dolls for their Lord and Master's amusement.

35. Some wives were used to show off their husband's wealth by wearing jewels, gold trinkets and embroidered gowns — conspicuous consumption.

36. But all wives had one main purpose: To bear sons to carry on the husband's name and inherit the property.

*The word family (*familia*) originally meant a man's slaves and included wives, children, concubines, servants, etc. Roman patriarchs ruled their *familia* with an iron hand — determining who would marry whom and when, how many wives to have, which children should live, etc. Infanticide usually by drowning or leaving unwanted or sickly babies out on a rock to perish has been a popular method of population control throughout human history.

37. Powerless, subject to arranged marriages, segregated and isolated in the women's quarters, subject to the whims of their fathers, their husbands, their brothers, their sons — women internalized their helplessness, their sense of inferiority.

38. Under the code of the "Three Obediences," Chinese and Vietnamese women had no control over their lives. As a child, a woman owed unconditional obedience to her father. When married, obedience to her husband, and when widowed, she was bound to obey her sons.

39. For almost one thousand years, Chinese mothers bound and crippled their daughters' feet — to tiny stubs with the rotting flesh sluffing off — leaving them unable to walk or to hobble, in great pain. *Why* did mothers do this to their daughters? In order to satisfy *a sexual fetish* of men who were turned on by small feet; mothers knew that the tinier the feet, the more likely the daughter could entice a rich husband.

40. As arranged marriages declined in Europe, girls competed with one another for husbands.

41. Middle- and upper-class "ladies" centered their lives on clothes, cosmetics, hairstyles, teas and corsets.

42. Men *and* women internalized these values: And, "It is hard to fight an enemy who has outposts in your head."*

43. It has taken a long time for us to challenge the double standard.

44. English Common Law decreed that married women had *no* rights. None. Zap. Zero.

45. They could not vote, they could not hold public office, they could not own property in their own name or control their own money — earned or inherited.

*Sally Kempton

46. They could not bring court suits in their own name or sit on juries.

47. They were effectively cut off from higher education and, often, from secondary education.

48. The first college to admit women was Oberlin. That was in 1833.

49. They were taught homemaking and teaching; but women students had special duties: "Washing the *men's* clothes, caring for their rooms, serving them at table, listening to their orations, but themselves remaining respectfully silent . . . being prepared for . . . motherhood and a properly subservient wifehood."*

50. English Common Law — under which married women had *no rights* — was brought to the American Colonies. A wife's inheritance, her wages, her home — belonged to her husband.

51. In the rare case of divorce, the husband automatically had child custody and all divorced women were considered to be low-status.

52. To be a divorced woman was to be a "fallen" woman; a woman without a man; a woman no longer a virgin; a woman of loose morals; a woman to be socially ostracized.

53. Women had *no* rights guaranteed them in the Constitution until 1920 when, after 72 years and hundreds of campaigns, they were "granted" suffrage.

54. When women in England finally won the right to vote in 1918, men could vote at age 21; women could not vote until they were 30.

55. The *sexual* double standard is, of course, the most glaring. A female is expected to be chaste; a male to play around.

*Eleanor Flexner, *Century of Struggle,* p. 30.

56. Go into any locker room as "Mr. Mucho-macho" proclaims, "Hey, guys, I made it with four different chicks last week!"

57. "Hey, man, way to go!"

58. "Super stud! Go get 'em, Tiger!"

59. "Romeo! Don Juan!"

60. "Play boy!"

61. Then watch what happens when a female says that she slept with four different men in one week. Watch the raised eyebrows; you can almost hear the words, the labels, going through people's minds — :

62. "Loose woman! Trash!"

63. "Slut! Whore! Tramp!"

64. "Nymphomaniac!"

65. "Promiscuous."

66. (Have you *ever* heard of a *promiscuous man*???)

67. ·Or, as my mother would say, "She's just *anybody's* girl!"

68. It's a double bind. Kate Millet asks: "Aren't women prudes if they don't and prostitutes if they do?"

69. And men have *always* had a double standard toward prostitution: Women get arrested, their customers go free.

70. (We know *who* made those laws!)

71. Egyptian law states that a man who is "caught with a prostitute" is not imprisoned; instead, *his testimony* is used to convict and imprison the woman!

72. Phyllis Chessler, in her book *Women and Madness*, exposed the double standard in mental health.

73. The double standard exists in wages: Why is it that a woman in the United States earns 59 cents for every dollar earned by a man?

74. The double standards in politics, religion, medicine, education and other basic institutions are well documented.

75. In the United States, elected representatives attest to the double standard in government: Bella Abzug (AB-ZUG) wore a hat on the floor of the House of Representatives so men wouldn't *assume* she was a secretary. Shirley Chisholm (CHIS-UM) says that she suffered more discrimination *as a woman* than as a Black person when trying to gain political influence.

76. Women constitute over 50 percent of the population in the United States: Why is it that there are only two women senators, out of 100? That's only 2 percent. And why are there only 23 women out of 435 members of the House of Representatives? That's less than 6 percent.*

77. Why is it that female-headed families are six times more likely to be poor than families headed by males?

78. Why is it that a government secretary is paid less than a government parking lot attendant, and child care workers' salaries are on a par with dog pound attendants?

79. Why is it that less than 3.6 percent of all grants go to women's projects?

80. Why is it that girls are treated differently and more harshly than boys by the juvenile justice system?

81. Why is it that one-fourth of all women experience some form of sexual abuse before the age of 18?

82. Why is it that by conservative estimates 1.8 million women are battered by their husbands?

*Change numbers when appropriate.

83. Why is it that women appear in only 31 percent of textbook illustrations, and then only as housewives, teachers or secretaries? *

84. Most of society's double behavior standards for women and men are covert — the results of very subtle conditioning. They are much more insidious and less tangible than, say, economic disadvantages.

85. It is the *subtle* socialization — the toys, the school counselors, the books — that tell little girls they should be nurses, while little boys are expected to become doctors.

86. The teachers who expect boys, *not* girls to be good at math.

87. The mothers who say "nice" girls *don't* climb trees and "boys-will-be-boys."

88. The cultural norm that expects women, *not* men to give up their careers for parenthood.

89. A husband who will "help" *his* wife with *her* laundry, *her* dishes, *her* household chores, *her* shopping, *her* dinner party...

90. These are some of the double standards that still permeate our society.

ALL READERS *(in unison)*:

> WHAT'S GOOD FOR THE
GOOSE IS GOOD FOR THE GANDER.
WHAT'S GOOD FOR THE GANDER IS GOOD FOR
THE GOOSE.

Readers sit down. READERS #6 & 7 *return center stage to read Part III, the continuation of "How to Tell A Businessman From A Businesswoman", dialogue 2.*

*(Feel free to add some current issue.)

PART III

DIALOGUE:

HOW TO TELL A BUSINESSMAN FROM A BUSINESSWOMAN, Dialogue 2

(for two readers)

READERS #6 & 7 *(the same woman and man who read Part I) return center stage. The man reads the title:*

BUSINESSMAN: How To Tell A Businessman From a Businesswoman.

BUSINESSWOMAN
points to BUSINESS-
MAN *and says:*

BUSINESSMAN *points to* BUSINESSWOMAN *and says:*

A picture of the family is on his desk: Ah, a solid, responsible family man. . . . .

The family picture is on her desk: Hmm, her family will come before her career.

His desk is cluttered: He's obviously a hard worker and a busy man. . . . .

Her desk is cluttered: She's obviously a disorganized scatter-brain.

He's not at his desk: He must be at a meeting. . . . .

She's not at her desk: She's probably gossiping with some other women.

He's not in the office: He's meeting customers. . . . .

She's not in the office: She must be out shopping.

He's having lunch with the boss: He's on his way up. . . . .

She's having lunch with the boss: They must be having an affair.

The boss criticized *him*: He'll improve his performance. . . . .

The boss criticized *her*: She'll be very upset.

He got an unfair deal: Did he get angry? . . . .

She got an unfair deal: Did she cry?

He's getting married: He'll get more settled. . . . .

She's getting married: She'll get pregnant and leave.

He's having a baby: He'll need a raise. . . . .

She's having a baby: She'll cost the company money in maternity benefits.

He's going on a business trip: It's good for his career. . . . .

She's going on a business trip: What does her husband say about that?

He's leaving for a better job: He recognizes a good opportunity. . . . . .

She's leaving for a better job: Women are so undependable.

He climbed the ladder of success. . . . .

I'll bet *she* slept her way to the top!

READERS #6 & 7 *sit down*. READER #1 *returns to center stage.*

PART IV

SKIT: THE BOSS

(a cast of three)

INTRODUCTION

READER #1: When confronted with an issue, the question I most often ask is, "Is it fair?"

Well, I am sure that the double standard is *not* fair.

I have often wondered what life would be like if men and women, through millenia, had lived as co-equals. What would life be like today had we developed an androgynous society?

And, I have sometimes wondered what society would be like if matriarchy — female rule — had evolved.

We invite you now to sit back and relax. Allow your imagination to flow as we take a comic look at how things *might* have evolved if women had taken the power.

Using satire — and patriarchal patterns — we bring you a modern matriarchy.

This skit is called . . . THE BOSS.

READER #1 *sits down as the cast of the skit, THE BOSS (READERS #8, 9 & 10) take their places.*

THE BOSS

a modern satire

—skit for a cast of three—

SETTING: Restaurant. Seated at a small table facing the audience are two middle-aged, middle-class professional women. They are "dressed for success" in chic, tailored business suits. They wear "proper" make-up, are neatly coiffed; they give the impression of an aura of "charm" and competence.

PROPS: Small table with white or red-checkered tablecloth.
Two chairs.
On the table are one martini and one whiskey sour glass.
Waiter can have a note pad and a pencil for taking the order, carry a small towel over his left arm and use a tray to serve the drinks.

CAST:

MARGE, a successful owner of a small, undefined business, who
    has been married to Harold for over 20 years; their children
    are grown.

JOYCE, a successful lawyer. Unmarried.

WAITER, played as a traditional waiter by a straight male with no
    swishy characteristics. He has no dialogue, but timing is
    crucial. (He may be played by a woman in a male suit such
    as a waiter might wear.)

Marge and Joyce are seated at the table. Marge is gulping her first double martini, while Joyce slowly sips her whiskey sour. Waiter is standing, waiting to finish taking Marge's order.

MARGE: Gawd! I needed that! *(To WAITER)* Let's see, steak, medium rare, baked potato, green salad . . . thousand island . . . and another double martini, very dry, and hurry with that drink, Honey. *(Winking at WAITER)* That-a-boy!

(WAITER exits. MARGE turns to talk to JOYCE)

My gawd, Joyce, ever since Harold took that course in French cooking, dinner has been sheer hell. Filet of sole with Mornay sauce, Chauteaubriand, aspics, crepe suzettes avec kirsch . . . My mouth simply waters for plain old meat and potatoes. *(To WAITER as he sets down martini glass).* Just in time, Sweetheart.

(MARGE swills down remains of the first drink. WAITER picks up the empty glass and exits. JOYCE is sipping on her whiskey sour.)

Joyce, for Christ's sake, when are you going to learn how to drink? *(Sarcastic.)* A whiskey sour's a man's drink.

(Taking a sip of her martini.) What a week! Hired a new receptionist.

JOYCE *(puzzled):*   Oh? A new receptionist? What happened to Larry? He's been with you for years.

MARGE: Oh, Larry is still with me. I couldn't get along without him. He thinks of everything, even corrects my spelling. Of course, he never lets me know — doesn't want to put a crack in my fragile female ego, you know . . . he's a real treasure. He even remembers to send flowers to Harold on his birthday and on our anniversary.

Business has been very good lately, so I thought I'd get some extra help for him . . . he is getting on a bit, you know, pushing forty. So, I hired Brian to answer the phones, make coffee, greet customers . . . take some of the load off Larry.

JOYCE: Sounds like a wonderful idea. So, what's the trouble, Marge?

MARGE: Brian disconnected me eight times this morning . . . during business calls! He simply cannot operate the phone panel. And the coffee . . . *(makes a grimace)* . . . yuk! It's swill, pure swill!

JOYCE: Why don't you fire him .
. . get a competent receptionist?

MARGE *(serious):* Mmmmm . . . maybe. *(Dawns on her.)* But
Brian is so cute! Simply oozes sex appeal. The customers
love him. He is rather a flirt, which doesn't hurt business.
Larry, dear love, efficient as he is, just doesn't have the old
S.A. — Sex Appeal, as they say.

JOYCE: How old is your new receptionist?

MARGE: Brian must be 21, or 22 max. *(Thinking.)* Nice tush . . .
great legs! Very mod and very revealing. *(Confidentially.)*
Joyce, you wouldn't believe it, but his clothes are sooo tight.
You can see practically everything, and I do mean
ev-er-y-thing!

JOYCE: Sounds disgusting.

MARGE: Oh, gawd, you're just like Harold . . . both so
puritanical.

JOYCE: Well, I just meant . . . Why don't you hire someone
who is competent, who can do the job?

MARGE: Oh, Joyce, it's obvious you've never owned your own
business. You've got to keep up with the times. Sex is in! It
titillates the customers, keeps them hanging in there . . .
more business.

(Pauses briefly, looks slightly reflective, and continues.)
Besides, he is cute. A doll. I'm thinking of putting the make
on him myself. Actually, he probably expects it . . . would
be insulted if I didn't at least make a pass. Grufff, just
looking at him makes my juices flow . . . and Hell, I'd trade
a lousy cup of coffee for a good lay any day! Wouldn't you?
But, enough of my problems. Tell me, how is the law
business?

JOYCE: Depressing. Five divorce cases this week. I don't know what divorced women expect . . . They don't want to pay spousal support, and very little child support. They truly expect their husbands to work eight hours a day at their jobs, come home, cook, clean, give full attention to the children, while they are free to come and go as they please. And yet these women still gripe about paying one-hundred bucks a month child support! Absolutely no sense of fairness or responsibility.

MARGE: Well, what do you expect, Joyce? You can't keep women tied to someone they no longer love or want . . . that wouldn't be fair either . . . After all, life is short. You've got to go for the gusto! Grab as big a piece of life as you can!

JOYCE: But, Marge, there has to be some sort of standard of decency, of love, of some real human relationship . . .

MARGE: Damn! You are like Harold. I come home exhausted from work and what does he want to do? Talk. TALK! Claims he needs to relate to me . . . exchange ideas, be an intellectual companion.

(Slowly.) All I want is a decent meal, a clean house, and some peace and quiet! That man drives me crazy, absolutely crazy!

JOYCE: I hear that Harold is very busy these days.

MARGE: Yes, indeed. Head of the Cancer Drive again. Fund raiser for the Alan Alda Household Melancholia wing at the new mental hospital. He's also taking a painting course. Actually, his watercolors are rather good. He might actually have some talent. He gave up his interest in Skinner* . . . Yeah, Harold's involved now in psychic phenomenon, E.S.P., crystals . . . that sort of thing.

JOYCE: Sounds exciting!

---

*Feel free to change to reflect your audience, e.g. "He gave up his interest in cultural anthropology . . . "

MARGE: What's exciting about being married to a middle-aged menopausal mystic? But, come to think of it, it's preferable to Skinner and Pavlov* and all those behaviorists.

JOYCE: But, Marge, you should realize that Harold is very bright. He needs outside interests, some intellectual stimulation, especially since the children are now grown and gone.

MARGE: You sound like Harold. He keeps telling me he feels unfulfilled, like some sort of non-person, a mere adjunct to my existence. Joyce, last night he went on, and on, and on, until my head was splitting. Finally, I said, "Harold, why don't you give up your painting, your reading, your civic deeds, your charitable drives, and do something productive with your life for a change . . . Get a job!"

JOYCE: What did he say?

MARGE: Surprised me. Really. Said he had been looking for a job, but he didn't want to be just a receptionist or a secretary like Larry. Ha! He should have it so good! But no one will hire him for anything else. Well, he hasn't worked in twenty years, and at his age — he's 45, you know — no one is interested in him. And what he can do with a degree in Psychology**? He told me he's been looking for a job for almost a year . . . with no luck.

JOYCE: That's sad, but Harold is sharp. There are a number of Men's Re-entry Programs in the area.

*". . . it's preferable to Margaret Mead and Ruth Benedict and all those anthropologists."

**Feel free to change to reflect your audience, e.g. Anthropology, Sociology, English Literature. . .

MARGE: Hell, he doesn't need those. I provide a good living, a good home . . . What more does he need? You know, I really think he's ungrateful for all I've done . . . a damn malcontent.

(Pauses.) Frankly, Joyce, my idea of the perfect husband is a deaf mute* who's a damn good lay.

(Joyce is shocked.)

Oh, don't look so shocked. It's every woman's dream man . . . Anyway, to continue about last night. Finally, I just gave up. *(Angry.)* I was totally exasperated with him, and I told Harold I was sick and tired of his clitoris envy . . . and to go see Dr. Benson and get his hormone prescription refilled.

(Sees young men across the room; nudges Joyce's arm and points at them.)

Hey, Joyce, over there. Look at those two young hunks! That's what my new receptionist looks like. Wowie . . . . Foxxxy studs! Wouldn't you just love to get your hands on those pectoral muscles . . . the hip action ain't bad either!

JOYCE: Doesn't interest me. I'm not into the sex game any longer. I want something more lasting . . . a meaningful relationship. *(Deep sigh.)* And I think I've . . .

MARGE *(interrupts)*: Joycie, Sweetie, you're getting old too soon. Maybe you ought to see Dr. Benson and get a check-up.

(JOYCE just gives another slight sigh. MARGE is animated and points to young men across the room.)

Last year, I picked up one of those in a bar. What a night! He must have been a graduate of the Masters & Johnson clinic. *(Face lights up.)* Could he ever turn a gal on . . . really hung . . . a real man! *(Laughing.)* I was exhausted for two days afterwards.

JOYCE: Did Harold ever find out?

---

*We recognize this terminology may be offensive, but it is an appropriate comment coming from this sterotyped character.

MARGE: Yeah, I did stay out all night . . . and most of the next day. Harold cried, cried, cried. My gawd, turned on a damn faucet. "Harold," I said, "it was just a pick up . . . just a one-night lay . . . two ships passing in the night. It didn't mean a thing." Still he kept crying. I don't know, Joyce, men are funny. They just don't understand these things. Women were just not meant to be monogamous like men.

JOYCE: Oh, Marge, how could you! You said you'd be faithful after that awful affair with Harold's best friend.

MARGE: Awful affair! Joycie, I'll have you know that was THE affair of my life! Not at all like Harold, who tires too often, and then never varies his routine much. My gawd, Richard could not only get it up whenever I wanted it, but he could keep it up. . . all night! Even in his prime, Harold could never do that!

JOYCE: You are too hard on Harold. He's plenty sexy. Besides, all these years he has always been faithful and loyal to you, loving and caring, a good father, absolutely devoted to you . . . while you played around and broke his heart.

MARGE: Come off it, Joyce. Oh well, all right, Harold does have all of those qualities and he is a good father, but he's just NOT the same as when he was young. Have you noticed the crow's feet around his eyes? And the deep lines in his face? And last night I noticed his neck is even getting a bit crepy *(KRAY-PEE)*. He's no kid anymore.

JOYCE *(interrupting)*: But all of us are getting older every day . . . and, hopefully, maturing.

MARGE *(ignoring Joyce's interruption)*: And now, all that complaining about my not relating to him on a personal, human level . . . It's really all too much . . . a real drag. *(Leaning forward.)* Actually, I've been thinking of divorcing him . . . that's why I wanted to meet you for lunch today.

JOYCE: I can't represent you, Marge. I think you should know
that I find Harold utterly charming . . . a complete person.
In fact, *I've fallen in love with Harold.*

MARGE *(incredulous)*:   You and Harold are having an affair!!!

JOYCE: Yes, it just began. And, it is NOT an affair. I love
Harold and I think he is beginning to love me, too.

MARGE: You and Harold in love?

JOYCE: We enjoy each other.

MARGE: You and Harold?

JOYCE *(rising from the table)*:   Yes, Marge. I adore Harold. And
if you don't like it, you know exactly what you can do about
it. Good-bye! *(JOYCE leaves.)*

MARGE: Harold? MY Harold? *(Pause.)* Why, the old whore!
Joyce? Joyce and Harold? Well, if either of them thinks for
one minute they are going to get one cent of alimony out of
me after he has had the audacity to be so unfaithful, they've
both got another think coming! *(Pause.)* Why, the no-good
bastard! How dare he! Getting some on the side, while I
work and slave all day for him. The nerve of that ingrate!
Well, as I've said so often, *you just can't trust men . . .*
flighty . . . over-emotional . . . totally untrustworthy.
(Beckons to WAITER.)
Hey, handsome, I'll have another double martini . . . *(Sexy
tone as WAITER picks up empty martini glass.)* . . . and,
honey, very, very dry this time.

*(As the WAITER turns to get the drink, with a big smile,
MARGE gives him a soft pat on the fanny. The WAITER
turns around and MARGE puckers her lips and gives him
two air kisses. WAITER exits, shaking his head in disbelief
and disgust.)*

End of skit.

(All READERS of Parts II and V stand center stage.)

-124-

PART V

READING:

THE SUMMING UP

Readers stand and say in unison:

<u>ALL READERS:</u>   WHAT'S GOOD FOR THE GOOSE IS GOOD FOR THE GANDER.
WHAT'S GOOD FOR THE GANDER IS GOOD FOR THE GOOSE.

Cast can shake their index fingers toward the audience on the last four words.

1. I doubt that a matriarchal society would have evolved this way.

2. Most women really aren't like men.

3. We have to be careful, though, especially women climbing the corporate ladder — learning games mother never taught her — mean, nasty, manipulative games.

4. As women achieve equal rights and freedom, they have to be careful <u>not</u> to become like Marge.

5. Patriarchal values *are* hazardous to our health.

6. Oh, "We've come a long way, Baby!" And now women have the lung cancer to prove it. Today, more women are smoking than men.

7. When women buy into patriarchal values, rates of heart attacks, ulcers, strokes and other stress-related illnesses increase.

8. Do women *want* to pattern themselves after the patriarchy? Fall into the male trap? Locked into a job? The treadmill? The machismo (MAH-CHEEZ-MO) competition? Blindly acceding to male standards?

9. Unable to cry, or to express feeling? Dying ten years too early?

10. No, I think not. Women are learning to be assertive, *not* aggressive.

11. Women are learning to be successful without losing their femininity; without losing values of caring, of tenderness, and of creating warm, supportive environments.

12. Women *are* humanizing the workplace, and we must continue to initiate and support flex-time, shared jobs, stress-reduction classes, gyms and exercise on the job site.

13. There is much more to do: Good 24-hour child-care centers.

14. Comparable worth (pay equity) is an important issue — for without economic security, options are limited.

15. We must have shared responsibilities — and joys — at home. Working mothers *and* fathers must share household chores *and* child-rearing.

16. Unfortunately, working women throughout the world are still expected to do the shopping, the cooking, the cleaning *and* the child-care; they work eight or more hours a day and then another four hours when they get home — the old double-standard.

17. No, we don't want to be caught up in a competitive, exploitive society.

18. We don't want high blood-pressure, heart attacks, ulcers, lung cancer.

19. We want to create a world where we can work and live in a healthy, peaceful environment...

20. Women do *not* want to change places with men.

21. Or to reverse the roles of men and women.

22. Or to oppress or dominate men.

23. Or to become less feminine.

24. But to participate more fully in the creation of a society where being born a woman is *not* a losing proposition.

25. Women want to work and live in a society where both women and men have an equal chance at winning.

26. Women want options and opportunities — and an end to the double standard.

27. Women want an end to traditional stereotyped sex roles which have — through the centuries — circumscribed both women and men.

28. We *will* put it all together and we *will* move ahead so that *everyone* benefits.

29. As the double standard fades into history there is emerging *one* standard — a standard of respect, dignity, equality and love for *all* people, men *and* women, boys *and* girls.

30. A standard where each of us can be ourselves.

31. A standard of equality.

32. Where both women and men can express feelings, can cry, can hug, can be nurturing and tuned into their feelings — as well as utilize their intellect and their skills.

33.   A standard of being fully human.

<u>ALL   READERS</u> *(in unison)*:   WHAT'S GOOD FOR THE
GOOSE IS GOOD FOR THE GANDER.
WHAT'S GOOD FOR THE GANDER IS
GOOD FOR THE GOOSE.

*Readers sit down. READERS #6 & 7 return center stage to
read Part VI, the conclusion of "How to Tell A Businessman
From A Businesswoman," dialogue 3.*

❖❖❖❖❖❖❖❖❖❖❖

> *"A woman should not be a
> mirror image of man's universe.
> A woman should not try to
> emulate men, thus taking on
> masculine traits, she should deve-
> lop herself, realize herself, gain
> direct vision into her own being."*
> —Anais Nin

> *"Women are still occupied in
> making the world as the man
> wants it, and then trying as best
> they can to create one they can
> breathe in."*
> —Anais Nin

PART VI

DIALOGUE:

HOW TO TELL A BUSINESSMAN FROM A BUSINESSWOMAN, Dialogue 3

(for two readers)

Readers (–6 and 7) — *the same woman and man who read the DIALOGUE, parts 1 and 2 return center stage. The man reads the title.*

BUSINESSMAN: How To Tell A Businessman From a Businesswoman.

Woman *points to* man *and says:*	Man *points to* woman *and says:*
A businessman is aggressive ...	*A businesswoman is pushy.*
A well dressed businessman is *fashionable*	A well dressed businesswoman is a *clotheshorse.*
A businessman is good on *details.*...............	She's *picky.*
He's depressed (or hung over), so everyone *tiptoes* past his office	She's moody, so it must be *her time of the month*!
He's a stern taskmaster	She's difficult to work for.
He *isn't afraid* to say what he thinks...............	She's *mouthy.*
He's *discreet*	She's *secretive.*
He's *over-reacting*	She's *emotional.*

He's *enthusiastic*.	She's *emotional*.
He weighs the facts and makes a decision that is *right*	She has *blind luck*.
He has grey at his temples; see how *distinguished* he looks	She's getting grey; see how *old* she looks.
He married a woman twenty years younger; such a *handsome* couple	She married a younger man; she *must* have money!

Both readers: WE HAVE BOTH BEEN 'DOUBLE CROSSED BY THE DOUBLE STANDARD.'
WOMAN: Remember what's good for the goose is good for the gander.
Man: What's good for the gander is good for the goose.
Both: DON'T YOU BE DOUBLE CROSSED BY THE DOUBLE STANDARD!

PART VII. *(Optional)*

AN EXPERIENCE IN AWARENESS

(Visualization/Guided Imagery)

If you have time, you may wish to include the following experiential process. So far, the program is about forty minutes long. **An Experience in Awareness** will add about ten minutes plus any discussion thereafter. You may, of course, shorten this reading.

Purpose: To increase awareness of how culture, language, thoughts and feelings come from a **male** point of view.

Directions: *Ask participants to get comfortable in their chair or lie down on the floor; to really settle in and relax.*

Announce: "We are now going to do a visualization. Please get comfortable in your chair (or lie down on the floor); really settle in and relax."

In a quiet voice, say: "Relax your hands, your arms, your shoulders, your neck muscles. Let the tenseness go. Just relax. Good. Relax your jaw, your facial muscles. That's right, just relax. Take a deep breath and allow your eyes to close. Relax your chest, your hips, your legs and your feet. . . good. Just relax and let the air breathe for you. Good. *(pause)*

"To continue the idea of reversing gender, I am now going to guide you through **An Experience in Awareness**, a visualization/a guided imagery/a fantasy of how things **might** have been if **women** had the power, if **matriarchy** - instead of patriarchy - had evolved.

"Just relax, let your eyes remain closed, and allow your imagination to flow as I read:

WOMAN   (WHICH INCLUDES MEN, OF COURSE) AN EXPERIENCE IN AWARENESS

1. I want you to consider reversing the generic term Man - to Woman. Recall that everything you have ever read or heard all your life used only female pronouns - she, her - meaning both girls

and boys, both women and men. At Christmas time people say, "Peace on Earth - Good Will Toward Woman" and holiday cards read "Peace To All Womankind." People talk about "The Sisterhood of Woman"; and in February we observe **Sisterhood Week.** Feel into that, sense its meaning to you.

2. And people talk about "The Future of Woman" which, of course, includes both women and men. Think of it as always having been that way, every day of your life. Feel the everpresence of the word "Woman" and feel the non-presence of the word "man." People read *The Descent of Woman,* anthropologists study *Pre-historic Woman,* and historians study *The History of Woman.* Absorb what it tells you about the importance and value of being woman (and of being man).

3. Recall that most of the voices on radio and TV are women's voices. It's women you watch and listen to when important news events are covered, on commercials, and on the late-night shows. **All women.** And, of course, films are directed and produced by women. . . and star women. And television news coverage is directed by an anchorwoman.

4. Recall that there are only two male senators in Washington, D.C. and out of 435 members of the House of Representatives only 23* are men. Our president is, **of course**, a woman. The vice-president is a woman. The attorney-general is female. The governor is a woman. **All women**. It has always been that way.

5. Feel into the fact that **women** are the leaders, the power-centers, the prime-movers. In the United Nations. In labor unions. In industry and business. **All women.** Man, whose **natural** role is husband and father, fulfills himself through nurturing children and making the home a refuge for woman. This is only natural to balance the biologic role of woman who devotes her **entire** body to the race during pregnancy.

6. Then, feel further into the obvious biological explanation for women as the ideal leader - her **genital construction**. By design, female genitals are compact and internal, protected by her body, by Mother Nature. Male genitals are so exposed that **he** must be protected from outside attack to assure the perpetuation of the

These figures (hopefully) will increase over the years.

human race. His **vulnerability** clearly requires sheltering. As children, girls are free to roam and explore and create. . . and be naughty. For, after all, girls will be girls! Furthermore, men **cannot** tolerate pain like women and they die younger; **clearly,** they need the protection of women.

7. Thus **by nature,** males are more passive than females; they psychologically yearn for protection and feel exposed and vulnerable when they don't have a woman to take care of them. If a male **denies** these feelings, he is unconsciously rejecting his masculinity and his therapist (a woman, of course) will invite him to get in touch with the "child" in him. He remembers his sister jeering at his **primitive genitals** that flop around foolishly. His sister could run, climb and ride horseback unencumbered. Since she was free to move, she was encouraged to develop her body and mind in preparation for her active responsibilities of adult womanhood. The male vulnerability needs female protection, so he was taught the less active, caring values of homemaking. She excelled in sports; he was the cheerleader.

8. And, because of his *clitoris-envy*, he learned to strap up his genitals and be ashamed of them. He was *encouraged* to dream of getting married, waiting for the time of his fulfillment; he learned to be **coy** and **cute** and **pretty,** dependent and cuddly so that a woman will ask him for his hand in marriage, and his mother will give him away at the ceremony. **Of course,** he will take his wife's name and his **greatest joy** will be when a **girl-child** is born to carry on the family name. He knows that if it is a boy-child he has failed somehow - but they can try again.

9. The newspapers and the TV abound with girl's sports; women athletes earn very large salaries. In the art galleries are many pictures of frontal **male** nudes; **female** nudity is almost taboo. Women, being capable of almost unlimited sex, are the sexual aggressors - they ask men for dates. They "play around". Of course, **decent** men **are** not promiscuous. Women have the money to pay for sex; **male** prostitution abounds. When there's an arrest, it is the male prostitute, **not** the female customer, who goes to jail.

10. All religions worship the Great Mother and pay homage to the Goddesses. **Women** are in the pulpits; men prepare church suppers and the rummage sales. **Women** sit on the Boards of multi-national

corporations. **Women** are university presidents and college professors; men teach elementary school.* **Women** are doctors; men are nurses. **Women** have the money! **Women** make the decisions! It's a **woman's** world!"

Directions:

In a quiet voice, say: "Please, now come back to this room; the visualization is over and you feel relaxed and good about yourself. When you are ready, allow yourself to open your eyes, and to yawn, and to take a big stretch. That's right, just raise your arms and have a big stretch. Put a smile on your face knowing that you have shared a unique experience with everyone here - an experience in sex role reversal.

"If you wish, please share with the group what you experienced. Could you relate to this guided imagery? Was your consciousness raised in any way?"

Discussion.

Depending on your audience, you may wish to add any of the following:

Women are presidents of banks; **men** are tellers.
Women administer community agencies; **men** are social workers.
Women design and build houses; **men** hire out as day workers
to clean other people's houses.
Women are engineers; **men** are receptionists.
Women are astronauts; **men** are programmers.
Women own and direct businesses; **men** are sales clerks.
Women run police departments; **men** are meter-maids.

OPTIONS *(Visualization):*

For a psychology class, for example, you may wish to read 6a, 7a, and 8a following number 6, and then continue with number 8.

6a.

Thus, **by nature,** males are more passive than females; during sexual relations they wish to be symbolically engulfed by the protective body of the woman. Males psychologically **yearn** for this protection, **fully** realizing their masculinity at this time - feeling exposed and vulnerable at other times. The male is **not** fully adult until he has overcome his infantile tendency to penis orgasm and has achieved the mature surrender to the testicle orgasm. He then feels himself a "whole man" as he is engulfed by the woman.

7a.

If the male denies these feelings, he is unconsciously rejecting his masculinity. Therapy is thus indicated to help him adjust to his **true** nature. Of course, his therapy will be administered by a woman for **only she** has the education and wisdom to facilitate openness leading to the male's growth and self-actualizations.

8a.

To help him feel into his defensive emotionality he is invited to get in touch with the "child" in him. He remembers his sisters jeering at his primitive genitals that "flop around foolishly." She can run, climb and ride horseback unencumbered. Since she is free to move, she is encouraged to develop her body and mind in preparation for her active responsibilities of adult womanhood. The male vulnerability needs female protection, so he is taught the less active caring values of homemaking. She excels in sports; he is the cheer-leader.

END

Scottish Dictionary: Honest
If he married her, he is said to "make an honest woman of her." —Jamieson
(1825)

AN EXPERIENTIAL PROCESS
Visualizing Yourself As A Different Sex

Purpose:

To develop awareness of how it would feel to be a different sex.

Directions:

Please sit with your feet flat on the floor and allow your hands to rest comfortably and open on your lap. Take a deep breath and relax. *(pause)* Now, breathe in through your nose and exhale through your mouth. Nice deep breath. Good. Allow your shoulders to relax. Allow your neck muscles to relax. Let the tension flow out of your body. Good. Gently allow your eyes to close and settle comfortably into your chair. Just relax your arms. Relax your hands. Relax your torso. Relax your legs. Relax your feet. Good. Allow your body to breathe for you. Relax, this will take only a few minutes. Good.

Visualization:

Now, I want you to imagine that your sex is reversed. If you are female, you are now a male. If you are a male, your body is now female. How is your body different now?

Become really aware of this new body, particularly the parts that have changed. In your mind's eye, look down at your new body. Look at your new arms, your new chest, your new hips, your new pelvic area, your new legs. Good.

Now, in your mind's eye go to a mirror and look at your new face. Look at your new body. How do you feel in this new body? *(pause)* Start to walk - Yes, take some steps in your new body. How has your walk changed? Now, find a comfortable chair and sit down in your new body. Are you sitting differently? Relax and think about how your life will be different now. What will you do differently, now that your sex has changed? *(long pause)* And, how do you feel about these changes? *(pause)*

For those of you who can visualize your new body, continue to explore your experiences for awhile. . . and, if some of you don't want to do this exercise, that's okay. But don't say to yourself, "I can't do this." Say, instead, "I won't do this", or "I choose not to do this" and add whatever words come to you next. By doing this, you may get some idea of what it is that you are avoiding by refusing to do this sex reversal process.

For those of you who are experiencing your new body, allow yourself now to dress your new body. What clothes are you selecting? *(pause)* Put on your underwear. Now, your outer garments. What parts of your body are uncovered? What parts of your body are covered? Look down at your shoes. What color and what style are your shoes? Do your clothes feel different? Are the colors different for you? Now that you are dressed, take a walk downtown or to a shopping center. *(pause)* Walk by a department store and see your reflection in the window. What do you see? Do you like what you see? *(pause)* Walk again. How do you think other people see you while you're walking? Do you feel attractive? Do you feel safe? Do you feel strong? Do you feel sexually attractive? *(pause)*.

It is time now to change back and get in touch with your real body and your real sex. Yes, change clothes and get back into what you were wearing when we started this process. Good. Now that you are back into your real body and the clothes you were wearing when we started this visualization, what did you experience as the other sex that you don't experience now? *(pause)* Were these experiences pleasant or unpleasant? Continue to explore your experience/your visualization for a little while. *(pause)* Yes, compare your body now and how it was as the opposite sex. Good. *(pause)*.

Now, come back to this room at this time and slowly allow your eyes to gradually open. Take a nice deep breath and then raise your arms to stretch. Good. *(pause)* You feel happy and rested and relaxed. In fact, you feel better than you've felt in a long time.

Now, please share with us your experiences in visualizing yourself as a different sex. Was it fun? What happened?

Or, you may wish to have participants write down the highlights and nuances of their experience.

PART VIII *(Optional)*

Discussion:

Discussion after the dramatic reading might include:

1. Has anyone in this room experienced the double standard? Describe.
2. How do women suffer from the double standard?
3. How do men suffer from this double standard?
4. How do men benefit from the double standard?
5. How do women benefit from the double standard?
6. What would the world be like if there were **no** double standards?

If we have come to think that the nursery and the kitchen are the natural sphere of a woman, we have done so exactly as English schoolchildren come to think that a cage is the natural sphere of a parrot - because they have never seen one anywhere else.

-George Bernard Shaw (1891)

---

*In no other aspect of sexual behavior is the **double standards** more vicious than in the "conflict" between heterosexuals and homosexuals. This "conflict" is commonly presented in terms of **normalcy versus deviancy**, but this framework itself is a propaganda success of heterosexuals. What is universal or "normal" in human sexual behavior is for two persons to need each other for mutual sensual enjoyment. Nothing in "human nature" requires that two persons engaged in such pleasure be of different sexes. Human beings are human beings, and however they mutually agree to please, comfort, inspire, or love each other is of human value.*

A LETTER TO A MAN

Do you know a man involved in work that requires the effective use of language, a man who can be relied on for intelligence and fairmindedness? If so, please pay him the compliment of sending him this letter.

Dear _____

You have been chosen to receive this message because you have shown yourself to be one of the more intelligent, open minded, and responsible people among those with special power to influence others by the use of words.

You have demonstrated a sensitivity to the great but often subtle powers of language over people's minds.

No doubt you perceive to an uncommon degree that the language of a people matches and reflects their whole social structure.

Sexism permeates our language to such an extent that it requires a whole relearning process to speak and write without constantly relegating the female sex to an inferior status.

For instance, it is of course simply not true - and never was true - that the word "man" "used generically" means exactly what it says - that women don't really count, that they may be subsumed as adjuncts, part of "man's" domestic impediments.

The use of the word in this way accurately reflects a social reality that must be changed.

Likewise, the use of such expressions as "mankind," "mastery" of a subject, "crafts**man**ship," "brotherhood," "chairman," etc. simply discount women as human beings.

Even the use of the masculine pronoun in all cases except where the referent is explicitly female expresses the general assumption that the standard for representing humanity is the male.

If you have a good imagination and some understanding of psychology, you, as a man, can gain insight into the female experience of language in patriarchal society by reading the following paragraphs thoughtfully and feelingly.

You are a man.

Suppose your name were John Annsdaughter, while several of your buddies at various times in your life had names such as George Sarahsdaughter, Harry Janesdaughter, etc.

Suppose you have grown up speaking a language in which the so-called generic term meaning a human being is "woman."

All through school you have read books about human society

(almost all written by women) with titles such as *The Family of Woman, A History of Womankind, The Ascent of Woman, The Religious Woman, Woman and Her Gods, Woman the Philosopher, The Image of Woman in Art Through the Ages, etc.*

Repeatedly, you read and hear that the most highly developed and powerful of beings on earth is Woman.

All your life you have learned about the amazing achievements of woman and also about her frightful capability of destroying anything she perceives as getting in her way.

The Constitution of your country reads: "We hold these truths to be self-evident; that all women are created equal. . ."

You sing a favorite national anthem: "America, America, God shed Her grace on thee and crown thy good with sisterhood from sea to shining sea."

You are to understand that you, as a man, are included in this "generic' use of female words.

Are you really convinced?

If you become really good at some job, you may be said to have mistressed it.

If you acquire skill in a craft you can become a craftswoman.

The Department of Labor will list your contributions under "Womanpower."

If you have a genius, you could even produce a mistresspiece; though, as you are a man, that's not considered likely.

In some organizations it may be possible for you to attain the honor of being a chairwoman; though, of course, you will never be the President of the nation; such exhalted offices have always been held exclusively by women (**not** in the generic sense).

Moreover, churches of all faiths regard only women as suitable religious leaders, since God's chief representatives here on earth have been females, as, morally, you may be praised for your femininity (word derived from the Latin "femina," meaning "woman" - instead of "virtue," a word derived from the Latin "vir" meaning "man").

In fact, rather ironically, you have always been made to feel that femininity is more important for men to have than for women; it requires self-abnegation and consists largely in playing an unobtrusive second fiddle.

When you read, though, that a good citizen will not let a rainstorm prevent her from getting over to her precinct to cast her vote, do you, as a man, really feel that the "good citizen" referred to is yourself?

The candidates, of course, are mostly women.

Your daily newspapers and news magazines contain about 9/10 news about women, written by women.

On TV you see 7 or 8 women for every man featured.

Most books and plays are mainly about women and their concerns, with men in supportive or subordinate roles.

At school, the history you studied was mostly about conflicts between women and groups of women, and the short lived if long-winded, settlements of those conflicts.

You also studied a lot of literature by women, a minute amount by men.

You studied almost exclusively women's philosophies, women's theories of religion, and women's theories of human psychology, all treating men as, by their nature, enigmatic, unpredictable, unreliable, and, at best, disconcerting if taken seriously.

Wise women regard men with a kind of tender amusement.

I believe you, as a fairminded man, would consider it improper, ill bred, or stupidly tactless to use racist modes of expression, language that's a put-down of blacks or orientals or other races.

Yet, you constantly use language in a way that's a put-down to one half of the human race.

Yes, it does take alertness, sensitivity and extra effort to reword your ideas so as to avoid sexist images; but doesn't it seem to you that a fairminded man should want to be in the forefront in the effort to eliminate sexist usages from our language?

We trust that you take justice seriously enough to want to make this effort.

That's why we are writing to you.

Yours sincerely for equality,

> "Women are not intrinsically, personally, and naturally inferior - their roles are inferior."
> Yolanda and Robert Murphy
> **Women of the Forest**

Have You Ever. . .

Wished you had longer legs?
Wished you were thinner?
Wished you were heavier?
Pretended you were dumber than the man you were with?
Lost a game with a man even though you knew you could win?
Admired your father's values and lifestyle more than your mother's?
Fantasized being carried away by a handsome prince?
Put your mate through college?
Faked an orgasm?
Submitted to sexual advances when you really didn't want to?
Wished you had bigger breasts?
Wished you had smaller breasts?
Wished you were a boy?

Had violence done you by a man?
Worked in an office/company where all the men were employers, all the women employees?
Worked full time, gone to school, been a homemaker simultaneously, by yourself?
Purchased and prepared food that the family liked rather than what you liked?
Denied the company of a woman to be with a man?
Had an abortion?
Been unhappy about being pregnant?

Earned money typing?
Been in a position to hire or fire a man?
Been a full-time homemaker?
Started your career as secretary, nurse or teacher?
Considered your career or your education secondary to your husband's?
Made a sexist statement to your daughter?

Do You Believe This?

It is only when a woman surrenders her life to her husband, reveres and worships him, and is willing to serve him, that she becomes really beautiful to him . . . the husband is king, and his wife is queen . . . it is the king who makes the final decision . . . What if the king makes the wrong decision? . . . The queen is still to follow him, forthwith . . . even though at times she desperately may not want to. He in turn will gratefully respond by trying to make it up to her and grant her desires. He may want to spoil her with goodies.

-Marabel Morgan, *The Total Woman*

Cooking three meals a day, washing that never ends, housecleaning that keeps repeating itself. When a woman has patiently performed these tasks for years, she is certainly a better woman because of it.

-Helen B. Andelin, *Fascinating Womanhood*

---

*There is a **double standard** of mental health - one for men, another for women - existing among most clinicians . . . For a woman to be healthy, she must "adjust" to and accept the behavioral norms for her sex - passivity, acquiescense, self-sacrifice, and lack of ambition - even though these kinds of "loser" behaviors are generally regarded as socially undesirable (i.e., non-masculine).*

-Phyllis Chesler
Women and Madness

We see with the eyes
of our culture.

What is, is presumed to be normative.

Culture is not only our creation but our creator.

I Wish I Knew
How It Felt To Be Free

I wish I knew how it would feel to be free.
I wish I could break all the chains holding me.
I wish I could say all the things that I should say.
Say them loud, say them clear
    For all the world to hear.

I wish you could know what it means to be me.
Then you'd see and agree
    That everyone should be free.

I wish I could give all I'm longing to give.
I wish I could live like I'm longing to live.

Well, I wish I could fly like a bird in the sky.
How sweet it would be if I found I could fly.

I'd soar up to the sun and look down at the sea.
Then I'd sing 'cause I know.
Then I'd sing 'cause I know.
And I'd sing 'cause I know, I'd know how it feels.

I'd know how it feels to be free.
Yes, I'd know how it feels.
Yes, I'd know, I'd know how it feels.
How it feels to be free.

Nina Simone, Victor (RCA) #1-4374
"I Wish I Knew How It Would Feel To Be Free."

We Might Come In A Fighting

Well we might come in a-fighting,
  Cause there's lots that needs a right-ing,
We've learned alot from liv-ing
  Never taught to us in schools -
If they say come in like a man
  Well, they must not understand,
When we enter in the game
  We-re gonna change the god-damned rules.
Well they say if you're living in a man's world
  There's got to be a boss,
  Someone giving orders
  Or it'll end in a total loss,
But we know just from liv-ing
  That all folks got stuff for giving,
Them hard line of authority
  We're bound to step across.

Chorus:
Well, we might come in a-fightin',
  Cause there's lots that needs a-rightin';
We've learned a lot from livin',
  Never taught us in schools;
If they say come in like a man,
  Well they must not understand,
When we enter in the game,
  We're gonna change the god-damned rules.

Well, they say if you enter in a man's world,
  there's got to be a boss,
Someone a-givin' orders,
  Or it'll end in a total loss;
But we know just from livin'
  That all folks got stuff for givin',
Them hard lines of authority
  We're bound to step across.

There somehow is this feeling
    We've got to work from nine to five -
Cause that's what makes a person,
    Worthy to be alive,
Yet most of what they're doin'
    Is bringing the world to ruin, -
Let's speed up on the living
    And slow down on the drive.

We Might Come in a Fighting

Words and Music by Carolyn McDade
© 1973 Hyannis Music

Well we might come in a-fighting, cause there's lots that needs a right-ing, We've learned a lot from liv-ing nev-er taught to us in schools-If they say come in like a man well they must not un-der-stand, when we en-ter in the game we-re gonna change the well they god-damned rules say if you're living in a man's world there's got to be a boss, someone giv-ing or-ders or it'll end in a to-tal loss, but we know just from liv-ing that all folks got stuff for giv-ing, them hard lines of bound to step au-thority we're a-cross.

Song: **"When A Man Wants A Woman"**

When a man wants a woman
He says it's a compliment
He says he's only trying to capture her
To claim her; to tame her
When he wants ev'rything ev'rything of her
Her soul, her love, her life forever and more
He says he's pursuing her
But when a woman wants a man
He says she's threatening him
He says she's only trying to trap him
To train him, to chain him
When she wants anything anything of him
A look, a touch, a moment of his time
He says she's demanding
He swears she's destroying him
Why is it
When a man wants a woman
He's called a hunter
But when a woman wants a man
She's called a predator

-Dory Previn

According to the law of Hammurabi (said to be the first written law, carved in stone about 1750 BCE): A man could divorce his wife by saying, "Thou are not my wife." However, a wife who used those words against her husband would be drowned.

Aristole could have avoided the mistake of thinking that women have fewer teeth than men by the simple devise of asking Mrs. Aristole to open her mouth.

—Bertrand Russell

Woman's place was in the home with the children. Domosthenes said: "Mistresses we keep for our pleasure, concubines for daily attendance upon our person, **wives** to bear us legitimate children and be our faithful housekeepers.While women were secluded to bear "legitimate children," men were out on the town having sex where they pleased. Euripides had Meadea say: "If a man grows tired of the company at home, he can go out, and find a cure for tediousness. We wives are forced to look to one man only." This was the **double standard** with a vengeance.

The double standard was instituted whereby a husband could have sex with any woman, but the wife was to be strictly monogamous.

Women came to be treated as property, the same as slaves and serfs.

Few societies have tried to impose rigid monogamy on males, but many have insisted on premarital virginity and marital chastity for women.

Specific source of the **double standard** lies in the partilineal patriarchal societies that ringed the eastern Mediterranean some 4,000 to 5,000 B.C.E.. Semitic peoples were nomadic so couldn't lock up women; they imposed swift physical punishment on the unchaste woman. She was stoned, or unless raped, usually strangled. Oftentimes she had to marry her rapist. Husbands had wide sexual liberties, but not with "good" women so a special class of "bad" women was created.

*The Victorians had needed to repress sexuality for the success of Western industrialized society; in particular, the total repression of woman's sexuality was crucial to ensure her subjugation. So the Victorian . . . supported by Freud, passed on to us the heritage of the **double standard.***

-Susan Lyndon
"The Politics of Orgasm"
Ramparts, Dec., 1968

*In society it is etiquette for ladies
to have the best chairs and get handed
things. In the home the reverse is
the case. That is why ladies are more
sociable than gentlemen.*

-Virginia Graham
Say Please

The Halacha (religious code of Judaism) does not recognize a woman as a witness of document signatory; the Islamic Law of Evidence defines one man's testimony as being worth that of two women; a Duke University study on courtroom testimony (in the U.S.) reveals that a woman's testimony carries half the weight of men's.

-Robin Morgan
Sisterhood is Global, p. 36

---

*If it's a woman, it caustic:
If it's a man, it's authoritative.
If it's a woman, it's too often pushy;
If it's a man, it's aggressive in the
          best sense of the word.*

-Barbara Walters

The history of woman is the history of the worst form of tyranny the world has ever known, the tyranny of the weak over the strong. It is the tyranny that lasts.

-Wilde
Woman of No Importance
Act III (1893)

Have you ever seen a man come up to four women sitting together in a bar and say, "Hey, what are you doing here all alone?"

-Lily Tomlin

Just as Booker T. Washington noted regarding the treatment of blacks by whites: "You cannot keep a man in the gutter without getting in the gutter yourself," so Robin Morgan notes: "Men will not be liberated until women are free."

*Society's **double behavior standard** for women and for men is, in fact, a more effective deterrent than economic discrimination because it is more insidious, less tangible. Economic disadvantages involve ascertainable amounts, but the very nature of societal value judgements makes them harder to define, their effects harder to relate.*

-Anne Tubker
The Woman's Eye
Introduction, 1973

The more "feminine" a woman's clothes are, the more circumscribed the use of her body.

WHY IS IT?

A man's grey hair is "distinguished"; a woman's grey hair is "Washed Out", drab and makes her look OLD?

Glasses on a man give an aura of intelligence, but men still don't make passes at women who wear glasses?

When a man is muscular he is strong; when a woman is strong she's obviously a dyke?

When a man doesn't talk, he's thinking; when a woman doesn't talk, she's being petulant?

When a man limps, it's an old war wound; when a woman limps, she's arthritic and crippled and ugly?

When a man forgets something, he's preoccupied; when a woman forgets something, she's an air-head?

When a man is irritated, it's called impatience; when a woman is irritated, she's a bitch.

When a man asks you to repeat something it's because he can't believe it; when a woman asks you to repeat something, it's because she's hard of hearing?

Militant Menopausal Woman

The core of this program is Marylou Hadditt's **Celebration of Mid Life and Menopause**. As we women from the First Unitarian Church of San Jose (calling ourselves Militant Menopausal Women) gave this dramatic reading to various groups we added a Prologue and an Epilogue. Feel free to add YOUR readings, poems and songs.

—Meg Bowman

ACKNOWLEDGEMENTS

My change of life was at Sonoma State University and with the people I met there. It is with deep appreciation and fondness that I recall them: Tak Richards, director of the Re-entry Students Center, for her ever-present encouragement and understanding. Remy Kingsley, Biologist and Counselor, for her guidance in the early days of this script. My housemate Kris Hill for being a careful reader and editor. Psychology professors Stashu Gertzen and Eliezer Pearson (may he rest in peace) for a classroom assignment from which Rights of Passage was born. Philosophy professor Stan McDaniel for helping me understand menopause as a re-birth process. 'Mac' McCreary for being there whenever I needed him. Lynn Waddington for pushing me to write when I didn't want to. And especially J.J. Wilson for believing in my capabilities.

My appreciation also goes to the women at Options For Women Over Forty in San Francisco for helping me work the kinks out of the script. Meg Bowman for her constant enthusiasm and for the candle-lighting ceremony which has been incorporated into the script. The Sonoma County Commission on the Status of Women for its Mid-Life Task Force. The women from all over who have written me letters and cards of encouragement.

And dear friends Anne, Carol, Dee, Jane, and Page - who helped me understand my change of life as a time for growth. I send them my love and thanks.

Marylou Hadditt

Militant Menopausal Woman

A program in ten parts for 6 women with suggested songs and optional materials.

Production Notes:

There are many options in presenting MILITANT MENOPAUSAL WOMAN.

Number of Readers; Although written for six women, the number of readers may vary from 3 to 8.

Props: All props are easy to acquire. If you elect to use a table as a prop to stand behind, decorate it with a lace tablecloth, three candles and some red flowers.

Ending: End with a chant and the introduction of the readers and/or a discussion on ageism. Or, throw red flower petals from a bowl or basket (on the table) into the audience. Or, end the program by having two readers each take a ball of red yarn from the table and "weave a web" amongst the audience.

Feel free to delete any part(s).

Although ageism and menopause are serious subjects, have fun with this reading. Let the ham out; it's okay to be silly. Hell, you only live once. Enjoy!

Meg Bowman

TABLE OF CONTENTS

Epilogue

(optional):

SONG OF THE MILITANT MENOPAUSAL WOMAN

Blues Singer sings or chants, like talking blues.
Singer claps her hands with the chorus and, if apropos,
may ask the audience to join her in singing the chorus
and/or clapping hands.

Or, begin with the entire cast speaking the chorus in unison:

> I'm a Militant Menopausal Woman
> A Worker, A Lover, A Wife.
> I'm a Militant Menopausal Woman
> 'Making myself a new life.

MILITANT MENOPAUSAL WOMAN BLUES

Words and music © by Marylou Hadditt 1980

Arranged by Steve Deutsch

I'm a mil - i - tant men - o - pausal wo - man, a worker a lover and a wife. I'm a mil - i - itant men - o - pausal woman and I'm making myself a new life oh yeah I'm making myself a new life

GROWING OLDER FEMALE (1980s)

Many older men and women face the problems of maintaining an adequate income to meet their needs for housing, food, clothing, medical care, transportation and to remain a part of the community. There is a difference, however, between older women and older men.

Let's look at the older population in terms of demographics: population, marital status, living arrangements and income, and let's review how society, in general, views older men and older women. In doing so, we can see the realities of growing older female.

Population: We older women far outnumber older men. More than sixty percent of all persons over sixty are women. Our life expectancy is eight years longer than men. This increased life expectancy has occurred in this century, primarily because medical science has helped us win the battle of surviving child birth. I believe men should look to curb their aggressiveness to increase their life expectancy.

Marital Status: The average age of widowhood is 56. By age 65, sixty-two percent of women are single as compared to twenty-three percent of men. Although there are more females over age sixty-five, there are nine times as many bridegrooms as there are brides. Most men marry within six to eighteen months following divorce or being widowed. Seventy percent of women remain single. Statistically, a woman should expect to spend the last fifteen to twenty years of her life as a single woman.

Living Arrangements: Eighty-eight percent of older men live in a family setting; the majority of women live alone. Over the age of seventy-five, three out of every four women live alone.

Income: There are vast differences between the incomes of older men and older women. One out of six elderly women lives in poverty (has an income of less than $5,600). This is due to lifetimes of unpaid work as a homemaker, or participation in underpaid occupations with only a one in five chance of receiving a pension, which in most instances is half of a man's pension. (The average pension one out of five women receives is $233 per monthj). Single women over the age of 65 have an income that is sixty percent of their male counterparts. (The median income for a single man is $10,000. per year; the median income for a single woman is $6,000.) Seventy-three percent of the elderly poor are women.

Social Security: Most women over sixty-five depend on social security as their only significant income (the average amount is less than $420. per month).

How does society "see" older women? There is a double-standard of aging. Men often become more distinguished, more powerful and more desirable as they grow older. Women become wrinkled, undesirable, indecisive drivers or they hold up traffic as they make their cane-assisted, frightened way across the street.

Organizations, such as the Older Women's League, have been instrumental in changing some pension laws, making minor improvements in the Social Security System, extending health coverage benefits and demanding research into medical problems affecting women. Attention is being centered on pay equity, job opportunities for mid-life and older women and recognition of the contributions of, and relief from, caregivers, be they young, mid-aged, or older women.

Personally, I'm one of the more fortunate older women. My health is good and I have a comfortable income. I live alone with its pluses as well as minuses. I am active in many organizations and I enjoy saying outrageous things, such as telling my oldest brother, when he asked why I hadn't remarried, that I wqill as soon as I find a man ten to fifteen years my junior who thinks I'm great. Well, HE married a woman fifteen years younger than himself! Of course, my new husband would have to realize that with the independence I've enjoyed living alone he'd have to assume the resonsibility for at least half of all shopping, cooking, and cleaning. And, he'd have to have a separate TV set outside of the living room for viewing all sporting events involving balls, hockey sticks or boxing gloves.

—**Charlotte Suskind**
1987

Suggestions for promotion:

Newsletter:

CELEBRATION OF MIDDLE AGE AND MENOPAUSE

"By facing her own emotion, love, fear, hate, whatever it may be, in stark reality, no longer camouflaged by the assumption of indulgence and maternal concern, she becomes once more one-in-herself, dependent only on the Goddess, truly a Daughter of the Moon."

-M. Esther Harding

Militant Menopausal Woman

(Date,time,place)
sponsored by

Hear the militant menopausal women
Workers - Mothers - Wives
The militant menopausal women
Makin' themselves a new life.

Hear women of all ages
Speak to us of life and death
Of dying and re-birth.

DRAMATIC CELEBRATION OF MIDDLE-AGE
A CELEBRATION OF MIDDLE-AGE AND MENOPAUSE

N.O.W. MEETING - WEDNESDAY 8 P.M.
(date and place)

PROGRAM

Suggested Program: This program is about one hour long. Feel free to change the suggested format, music, poetry, etc. to fit your time span and audience.

MILITANT MENOPAUSAL WOMAN
CELEBRATION OF MIDDLE AGE AND MENOPAUSE

(names)

REFLECTIONS ON MIDDLE AGE

WELCOME AND ANNOUNCEMENTS

OFFERTORY (if apropos)

POEM: 'Yes' For My Daughter, by Jean Embree

RESPONSIVE READING: 'When I Am Old' (adapted from poem 'When I Am An Old Woman' by Betty Mills)

(or) POEM: 'When I Am An Old Woman'

READINGS: 'Reflections on Middle-Age'
           Some Questions
           'We Live In A Youth-Oriented Culture'

CANDLELIGHTING

READING: 'Menopause'

DRAMATIC READING: 'Rights of Passage:
           A Celebration of Middle-Age
           and   Menopause'
           by Marylou Hadditt

SONG: 'Coming Home' by Carolyn McDade

LETTER: 'If I Had My Life to Live Over'
by Nadine Stair at age 85

CLOSURE: 'A Celebration of Middle-Age'

PROGRAM

The following are options which may be used as a preface to your program. If time is limited, RIGHTS OF PASSAGE: A CELEBRATION OF MID-LIFE AND MENOPAUSE by Marylou Hadditt can stand alone.

This program can be done in one or up to ten parts,e.g.:

PART I

POEM, such as **'Yes' For My Daughter**, Jean Embree, read by one woman.

PART II

SONG, such as **I Wish I Knew How It Would Feel To Be Free***
sung by the audience, choir, or group; or Nina Simone's recording can be played, or **Lydia Pinkham** (see p. 167). If sung by audience, copies of the song should be provided as well as an accompanist and leader.

PART III

RESPONSIVE READING, such as **When I Am Old**, adapted from **'When I Am An Old Woman'** by Betty Mills. Copies must be provided to the audience. If this is not desired or possible, a woman can read a poem such as **When I Am An Old Woman** by Jenny Joseph; **Menses: A Seasonal**, Pamela Victorine or **Gardener**, Erica Jong (p. 215).

PART IV

READINGS can include 'Reflections on Middle-Age,' 'Some Questions,' and 'We Live In A Youth-Oriented Culture,' each by a different reader. A jar of face cream can be used for illustration.

PART V

CANDLELIGHTING requires three candles, matches, an ash tray and three readers. A program could consist **only** of the candle lighting and the dramatic reading.

*Nina Simone, Victor (RCA) #1-4374

PART VI

READING on 'Menopause' by one reader.

PART VII

DRAMATIC READING, 'Right of Passage: a Celebration of Mid-Life and Menopause,' by Marylou Hadditt is read by six women. Women stand in back of a table and look at the woman speaking, not at the script. Each woman must have a script. We found it better not to try to dramatize, mime, or use gestures. If desired, one woman can sing or chant the 'Militant Menopausal Woman' blues at the beginning and at the end of the performance.

PART VIII

SONG, such as 'Coming Home' by Carolyn McDade can be sung by the audience, a choir, or a group. Audience must be provided with lyrics if they are to sing (p. 213).

PART IX

LETTER of Nadine Stair's, 'If I Had My Life To Live Over' by one reader (p. 214).

PART X

A READING, such as 'Let's Celebrate Middle-Age' (p. 216) or 'Growing Older Female' (p. 158) which can be revised to suit the audience. Part X can include a 'thank you' to the audience and to the cast.

NOTE:
At the end of part VII, of 'Rights of Passage: A Celebration of Mid-Life and Menopause,' by Marylou Hadditt, you may ask the cast of the DRAMATIC READING to introduce themselves.

SUGGESTED STAGE ARRANGEMENT

A CELBRATION OF MIDDLE AGE

' Candles		Lace Tablecloth
Matches	**TABLE**	Red Flowers
Ash Tray		Red Yarn

— Audience —

PROPS:

    1. Chairs for each reader, if desired.
    2. Table on which are placed:

        A. three unlit candles
        B. matches and ashtray
        C. if desired, a bouquet of flowers
        D. lace or crocheted tablecloth is optional
        E. a cosmetic jar
        F. red flower petals/red yarn (optional)

All women stand when reading the RIGHTS OF PASSAGE: A
CELEBRATION OF MIDDLE-AGE AND MENOPAUSE.

PROLOGUE

PART I

POEM

YES FOR MY DAUGHTER

It's getting to us, this whole women's lib-
Eration, liberty, the liberal pain:
The surgeon's knife is slicing at the rib
That never quite left Adam. Once again
We're being born, you and I, mother
And daughter. Each of us has stood in a dark
Year and fought the problem for the other —
The problem with no name — that brands the mark
Of battle in our minds. Now worlds of lives
Yawn before us like mouths of giants or bless
With widespread arms of love; which gate gives
Hope? Can each of us alone say yes
To life? Let's practice it as friends who love
Each other; then we can answer when worlds move.

—Jean Embree

PART II

Lydia Pinkham

Lydia Pinkham's "Vegetable Compound" was not the only hope for the women of the world. In France, for example, a certain Abbé Soury offered (at
seven francs a bottle) a "Youth Tonic" *("La Jouvence")* that guaranteed,
right on the label, to cure "diseases of the nerves and the stomach, blood
circulation troubles, feminine illnesses, discomforts of menopause, weakness,
neurasthenia, etc."

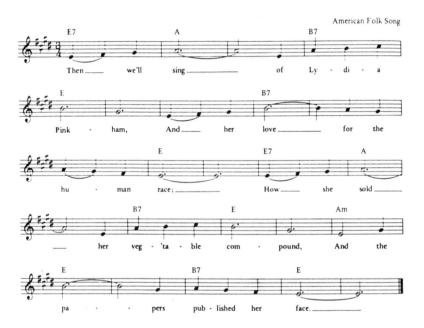

American Folk Song

Then ___ we'll sing ___ of Ly - di - a Pink - ham, And ___ her love ___ for the hu - man race; ___ How ___ she sold ___ her veg - 'ta - ble com - pound, And the pa - - pers pub - lished her face. ___

Oh, it sells for a dollar a bottle,
Which is very cheap, you see
And if it doesn't cure you,
She will sell you six for three. *Chorus*

Mrs. Jones, she had no children,
Though she loved them very dear.
So she bought some vegetable compound,
Now she has them twice a year. *Chorus*

PART III

When I Am An Old Woman

I shall wear purple
With a red hat which doesn't go, and doesn't suit me,
And I shall spend my pension on brandy and summer gloves
And satin sandals, and say we've no money for butter.
I shall sit down on the pavement when I'm tired
And gobble up samples in shops and press alarm bells
And run my stick along the public railings
And make up for the sobriety of my youth
I shall go out in my slippers in the rain
and pick the flowers in other people's gardens
And learn to spit.
You can wear terrible shirts and grow more fat
And eat three pounds of sausages at a go
Or only bread and pickle for a week
And hoard pens and pencils and beermats and things in boxes.
But now we must have clothes that keep us dry
And pay our rent and not swear in the street
And set a good example for the children.
We will have friends to dinner and read the papers.
But maybe I ought to practice a little now?
So people who know me are not too shocked and surprised
When suddenly I am old and start to wear purple.

From Warning
—by Jenny Joseph

WHEN I AM AN OLD WOMAN

When I am an old woman, I shall wear mostly jeans
And T-shirts that say outrageous things
And I shall spend my social security
On causes and   programs and books,
And say we've no money for appreciation dinners.
 I shall read Mad Magazine at public prayer breakfasts
And paste Abortion on Demand signs all over my car.
And put copies of the Humanist Manifesto in Gideon Bibles.
I shall take anti-draft resolutions
To the American Legion Christmas party
And make up for the caution of my middle age.
I shall plant daffodils in ditches
And only partonize service stations with petunias.
And continue getting brown and wrinkled in the sun.
I will quit cooking Mother's Day dinner
And cross out sexist words with red ink in library books
And leave parties when someone tells a sick joke on gays
And shoot holes in chauvinist billboards with my B-B gun.
But now I mustn't be pushy about women's rights
Or spoil everyone's good time by getting serious
And I must smile pleasantly at idiocy
And compromise truth with silence
And not offend someone
Who may be important to my husband's business.
But maybe I ought to practice a little now?
So people who know me are not too shocked and surprised
When suddenly I am old and start to wear T-shirts.

                                                        Betty Mills

Adapted from Jenny Joseph's poem. *(see page 168)*

WHEN I AM OLD

When I am old

I SHALL WEAR MOSTLY JEANS AND T-SHIRTS AND SAY OUTRAGEOUS THINGS.

When I am old

I SHALL SPEND MY SOCIAL SECURITY CHECK ON CAUSES AND BOOKS AND PROGRAMS.

When I am old

I SHALL READ MAD MAGAZINE AND PASTE ABORTION ON DEMAND SIGNS ALL OVER MY CAR.

When I am old

I SHALL PUT COPIES OF THE HUMANIST MANIFESTO IN GIDEON BIBLES AND TAKE ANTI-DRAFT RESOLUTIONS TO THE AMERICAN LEGION CHRISTMAS PARTY AND MAKE UP FOR THE CAUTION OF MY MIDDLE AGE.

When I am old

I SHALL PLANT DAFFODILS IN DITCHES, PATRONIZE SERVICE STATIONS WITH PETUNIAS AND CONTINUE GETTING BROWN AND WRINKLED IN THE SUN.

When I am old

I WILL CROSS OUT SEXIST WORKS WITH RED INK IN LIBRARY BOOKS AND LEAVE PARTIES WHEN SOMEONE TELLS A SICK JOKE ON GAYS.

When I am old

I WILL SHOOT HOLES IN CHAUVINIST BILLBOARDS WITH MY B-B GUN AND BE PUSHY ABOUT WOMEN'S RIGHTS.

But for now

I MUST NOT SPOIL EVERYONE'S GOOD TIME BY GETTING SERIOUS

For now

I MUST SMILE PLEASANTLY AT IDIOCY AND COMPROMISE TRUTH WITH SILENCE.

For now

I MUST NOT OFFEND SOMEONE WHO MAY BE IMPORTANT TO MY JOB OR MY HUSBAND'S BUSINESS.

But maybe I ought to practice a little now

SO PEOPLE WHO KNOW ME ARE NOT TOO SHOCKED AND SURPRISED WHEN SUDDENLY I AM OLD AND START TO WEAR T-SHIRTS.

Adapted from WHEN I AM AN OLD WOMAN *by Betty Mills, Unitarian from Bismark, North Dakota—which is based on Jenny Joseph's poem.* (see pages 168 and 171)

Meg Bowman

PART IV

READING(S)

'REFLECTIONS ON MIDDLE-AGE'

Old age? When is one 'old'? Middle-aged? When is one middle-aged? At 40? 45? The big 5-oh? Between 40 and 60? Whenever one feels middle-aged? No matter what our definitions are, aging is a privilege. A gift of the 20th century. And, it brings many challenges as our bodies and our roles change. Some people see middle-age as a time of growth. With the children gone, they renew their marriage. It's a time of travel, hobbies, growth. They remain active and positive. If they don't like their bed, they get up and re-make it...or, get another one. They explore options and alternatives. For others, middle-age brings anger and self-hatred; retirement brings boredom and loss of identity.

Today (tonight), we reflect on middle-age particularly as it affects women. We review the stages of our lives; and acknowledge menopause as a 'right' of passage. But first, we have some questions to ask.

'SOME QUESTIONS'

I have some questions to ask. We live in a youth-oriented culture. There is no council of elders. Forced retirement—being put out to pasture—is a fact of life. What would you do with the rest of your life? Where will you be when you're old? Thousands of older people, with frail health and lack of societal support, suffer their grim wait for death warehoused in filthy, cruel convalescent homes. WE MUST CHANGE THIS.

I HAVE SOME QUESTIONS TO ASK:

Why is the United Staes the only modern nation that doesn't assure their people security in their golden years? Think about it. In Canada, in Norway and elsewhere—older people are respected. Looked up to. Guaranteed a decent place to live, nutritious food and medical care.

I HAVE ANOTHER QUESTION TO ASK:

Why is the United States the only industrial nation—except for the Republic of South Africa—lacking a national health care system? Think about it...for someday (if we're lucky) we, too, will be old.

'WE LIVE IN A YOUTH- ORIENTED CULTURE'

Trying to 'look young' is a multi-billion dollar business. (*Hold up cosmetic jar*): This face cream promises to remove wrinkles— only $14.95 a jar. Need a face life? Six incisions, only $6,000. For a clear youthful skin. . . to remove those ugly brown age spots, use Pour-some-on-ya—use Its-so-dear-ica. . . Color your hair? Of course.

Let's have an end to supporting corporations who feed off our insecurities and our need to look younger. . . to look like the film star of the week.

Let's revel in and revere and retain our uniqueness, whatever our age. Let's love ourselves. Our marvelous bodies. Our humanness. Our age.

PART V

CANDLELIGHTING

Three women step forward and consecutively light a candle and read their part.

#1. I light this candle for all women who, through the eons, in many cultures, were segregated, scorned, cursed during their menstrual period.

#2. I light this candle for all post-menopausal women who were made to feel diminished, of little worth; that their life was over because they could no longer reproduce. The sad women who believed their only function was to bear and care for children.

#3. I light this candle for us: We who know that menstruation is normal, that menopause is a perfectly natural process. Women who demand choices, options...to choose how to live our lives: a worker, a mother, a wife...a militant menopausal woman.

Three candles are centered on a tablecloth, grouped with a bowl of fresh-cut red flowers. Women speak as they light the candles.

PART VI

'MENOPAUSE'

Menopause, often referred to as 'change of life' is that transition period from reproductive function to one of a more enlarged vista of activity. Most women have raised their children, gained a lifetime of trial and error experience, and are now ready to expand into new areas—

a new career
new enjoyments
new interests.

Menopause is a perfectly natural process. Another passage on life's continuum. We believe, as there should be a ritual acknowledging a young woman's start of menses—a womanhood 'right'—there needs to be a ritual acknowledging the onset of menopause.

Today (tonight), we bring you such a 'Right of Passage': A CELEBRATION OF MID-LIFE AND MENOPAUSE, written by Marylou Hadditt.

We bring you Militant Menopausal Women.

PART VII

RIGHTS OF PASSAGE

CELEBRATION OF MID-LIFE AND MENOPAUSE

by

Marylou Hadditt

Introduction

My menopause was a lonely time.

Back in the early 1970's, women weren't talking about menopause or about mid-life transitions. We were still tied down by our fears - afraid even to look at our own bodies and our own female functions. I clung to old wives' tales remembered from childhood. I never dared to voice my most secret fear: that, because my mother had died when she was only forty-one, I, too, would not live through menopause.

I had no idea what to expect from mid-life changes. When I missed a period, I thought I had somehow gotten pregnant. It took me a long time to find the courage to visit my doctor. He told me this was probably the beginning of menopause. I was forty-two at the time. When I asked him what I had to look forward to, his answer was vague and evasive. 'You could stop menstruating tomorrow or five years from now,' was all he said. I asked him about my severe depression, wondering if it could be related to diet or to hormonal changes. He replied that I should go into psycho-therapy. I didn't tell him I thought my three-day-a-week psychoanalysis was probably intensifying my depression.

The next five years were a nightmare for me. I was in and out of mental hospitals and psychiatrist's offices. Ultimately, I left my husband and my teenage daughters.

I have often wondered if this upheaval was symptomatic of my menopause. Now, almost ten years later I still cannot give a definitive answer. I can only report that, concurrent with the hormonal changes in my body, my life fell apart.

I survived. In fact, I have flourished.

At age 50, I began a new life, attending college for the first time. I have found satisfaction and contentment. After several tedious years, I began to feel good about myself with a confidence I had never before known. I wanted to celebrate. I sought some spiritual experience - I wanted to take part in a ceremony. I could find no ritual, no celebration, nothing for mid-life women either in current women's literature or in historical literature. I knew then that I had to create my own ritual celebration. Thus, the play Rights of Passage came into being.

Rights of Passage is a product of my five years at Sonoma State University in Northern California. Originally, it started as a guided fantasy in a Psychology class and was further developed into a short play as a term project for a Philosophy class. A version of this play was first performed by the Re-entry Students Association. We did an interpretive dance to the Ages of Woman, accompanied by guitar and recorder. We sang, chanted, laughed, and cried together.

We felt - and so did the audience - that we had made a beginning difference in the way women perceived mid-life and menopause.

Marylou Hadditt

This dramatic reading is for my three daughters, Gail, Lucia, and Penny. . . And for daughters, of all ages, everywhere.

CAST

#1. Mable—has a firm, loud voice and knows the tune to Major General's song from Pirates of Penzance.

#2. Gertie—has a firm, husky voice which can turn into a nasal twang.

#3. Grace—has facial wrinkles

#4. Has a dramatic flair

#5. Can do a sing-song voice

#6. An older woman

Nature intended women to be our slaves . . . they are our property; we are not theirs. They belong to us, just as a tree that bears fruit belongs to a gardner. What a mad idea to demand equality for women! . . . Women are nothing but machines for producing children.

-Napoleon Bonaparte

RIGHTS OF PASSAGE

Production notes:

Since the initial 1979 performance, **Rights** has been presented all over the country. Groups of women at conferences, meetings, retreats, and religious gatherings have found spiritual meaning and an expression of personal power in the play. Women have written me about there individual performances. One group used Chris Williamsons' "Sisters" from the album, **The Changer and The Changed**, Olivia Records; another used Kay Gardener's "Moon Circles" by Urania records. One group of performers wore full length flowered caftans; another matching red Tee-shirts. A woman's theatre group has named themselves Militant Menopausal Women Players, taken from the play.

Rights of Passage has been written for women of all ages; post-menopausal women, mid-life women, and women under thirty-five who will soon grow old. The play, which takes about forty minutes to perform, is designed to be read script-in-hand. There is little rehearsal time involved. One or two read-throughs should be sufficient. The stage directions are sparce because I envision **Rights** as a vehicle for each woman's individual and collective creativity.

Section One—THE AWAKENING

MILITANT MENOPAUSAL WOMAN CHANT

This chant is in the tradition of chanting folk songs or talking blues. The verses may be spoken or chanted by each individual woman while the chorus is chanted together by all the women, encouraging the audience to join in singing and hand clapping.

CHORUS
    I'm a militant menopausal woman
    A worker, a lover, a wife.
    I'm a militant menopausal woman
    Making myself a new life.

#1 WOMAN: They call me Menopausal Mabel
    Got rocks inside my head.
    Say I ain't really able
    To be much fun in bed.
    (What they don't know!)

#2 WOMAN: They call me menopausal Gertie
    Fill me up with es-tro-gens
    Doc says Honey this won't hurt ya'
    Just one or two car-cin-o-gins
    (Slow down, man, slow down!)

#3 WOMAN: They call me menopausal Grace
    Look young, girl, not your age.
    Take those wrinkles off your face
    They don't anticipate my rage.
    (You better believe!)

Repeat Chorus

#4 WOMAN: I'm a menopausal woman
And I'm a-growin' old
I can tell you things
Ain't never been told.

#5 WOMAN: So listen to me sister,
And listen, brother, too.
At fifty-one* I've got some stuff
I'd like to share with you.

#6 WOMAN: I'll tell you how a rose is cold
When you take it in your hand
And where the small sand dollar lives
Along the ocean strand.

I'll show you where the whippoorwill
Hides her song at close of day
And how sisters loving sisters
Will fade your fears away.

ALL WOMEN TOGETHER

Oh, we're getting older
It's made us kinda smart -
We've got a lot of learning left
And loving in our heart,
Because, y'see
 I'm a militant menopausal woman
A worker, a lover, a wife.
I'm a militant menopausal woman
Who's making herself a new life.

Repeat Chorus

(*) *Change to appropriate age.*

*All actors are seated. Musical transition is played. Suggested music is the first verse of "Changes" from the album **Mooncircles** by Kay Gardner, Olivia Records. This portion of the song is about two minutes long. When dancers are included, they enter here, dance and exit.*

Section Two—THE RAGE

The women rise with a sense of sadness. This chorus part is chanted in several voices, somewhat like a madrigal, with overlapping of lines. The duet keeps a steady rhythmical cadence, while the other voices overlap, but not enough so that the words become confusing to the audience. #5 woman's voice should speak above the duet: #2 woman should speak below. Each woman can alter the emphasis to suit herself, i.e., Mother NEVER TOLD ME. Or MOTHER never TOLD ME, etc.

#3 & #4 DUET: *(Chanting at a steady pace, droning, so involved in their own chant they do not hear the other voices).*

    My mother never knew
    My mother never told me

DUET: *(repeat)*

#5 WOMAN: Mother was afraid

#2 WOMAN: Mother didn't know

DUET: *(repeat)*

#5 WOMAN: Mother never told me

#2 WOMAN: Mother never knew

#1 WOMAN: I am afraid

DUET: *(repeat)*

#5 WOMAN: She didn't know

#2 WOMAN: SHE was ashamed

#6 WOMAN: I don't know

DUET: *(repeat)*

#5 WOMAN: Mother never told US

#2 WOMAN: WE don't know

DUET: *(repeat)*

#5 WOMAN: I am afraid

#2 WOMAN: I am afraid

#6 WOMAN: I am afraid

DUET: *(repeat) then, all six women in a stage whisper:*

CHORUS: *(stage whisper)* We are afraid

#1 WOMAN: *(with angry emphasis)* How could our mothers tell us when they didn't know? When our grandmothers were lucky to live to be fifty years old? At the turn of the century most women, at least those who survived after giving birth to eight or ten children, didn't live long enough to be middle aged. They didn't live to go through menopause.

#2 WOMAN: *(anger builds)* Our mothers were ashamed. The Victorians silenced all women. It was a time which led us to think that our bodies were dirty and evil. It was a time when women were ashamed of themselves and their physical functions. Menopause was hidden.

(Women are invited to insert their own experiences here)

Women speak these lines as much to one another as to the audience.

#3 WOMAN: Mothers didn't talk to their daughters and daughters didn't know.

#4 WOMAN: My mother gave me a book put out by Kotex. It talked about birds and bees, then said that Mary went to a party and didn't feel good. She came home and used Kotex. *(laugh sarcastically)*

#5 WOMAN: I thought I was bleeding to death.

#6 WOMAN: Mother said I couldn't go swimming.

#1 WOMAN: Mother wouldn't let me ride my bicycle.

#2 WOMAN: My mother slapped my face. She told me it was an old Jewish custom so I would always remember the day I became a woman.

#3 WOMAN: My mother said I was lucky to have Kotex. She used rags and had to wash them every day.

#4 WOMAN: *(painfully)* I didn't know what becoming a woman meant. I was pregnant at 14.

#5 WOMAN: *(with sarcastic disgust)* And I had to act like a "lady".

ALL WOMEN IN CHORUS: How could our mothers tell us when out mothers didn't know?

#6 WOMAN: They called menstruation THE CURSE.

#1 WOMAN: or wearing the rag.

#2 WOMAN: or being sick.

#3 WOMAN: or falling off the roof.

#4 WOMAN: They spoke in euphemisms. No one said the word blood. No one EVER said blood. No one ever said MENSTRUAL blood was the only blood which flows with never an injury. No one said that women's blood is the only blood which flows with NEW life. The word blood is unmentionable. The word blood is for men. For war and for violence.

#5 WOMAN: *(almost interrupting)* Bloody red on the TV and movie screens. Bloody red in unnecessary wars.

#6 WOMAN: Like our bodies, woman's blood was considered dirty and evil.

#1 WOMAN: Menstruation was taboo.

#2 WOMAN: And menopause was terrifying.

CHORUS:
>Our mothers never told us.
>Our mothers never knew.

#3 WOMAN: Our mothers whispered behind closed doors and tight corsets.

#4 WOMAN: They called menopause female trouble.

#5 WOMAN: Or the change.

#6 WOMAN: They didn't know what menopause was.

#1 WOMAN: They locked women in attics.

#2 WOMAN: And in asylums. They labeled menopause "involutional melancholia."

#3 WOMAN: They gave women shock treatments for menopause.

#4 WOMAN: My mother died at forty-two. I thought the change had killed her.

#5 WOMAN: Webster's New Collegiate Dictionary defines menopause as: "The final cessation of menstruation, occuring normally between the ages of 45 and 50." The word come from the Greek MENO meaning month and PAUSIS meaning to halt.

#6 WOMAN: Menopause marks the development to a stage beyond the reproductive cycle.

#1 WOMAN: It is completed when menstruation has stopped for twelve months.

#2 WOMAN: Menopause is a radical hormonal change, similar to adolescence. Sometimes some of us feel great turmoil. Sometimes some of us feel nothing.

#3 WOMAN: For decades manopause was taught to medical students as a hormone deficiency disease.

#4 WOMAN: But it's not a disease. The more we understand this, the better we can deal with it.

CHORUS:
> If we are to grow
> If we are to complete our lives
> We must welcome the dying-rebirth process
> Which is menopause

#5 WOMAN: One thing we can do is help each other understand the life process so we can approach mid-life and menopause with knowledge and without fear.

CHORUS:
> Listen. Listen to the crones.

#6 WOMAN: Anna, healer and holy woman from Holland believes that menopause is a special time for women to change any karma they did not resolve in adolescence. Menopause is an opportunity to discard old angers and guilts. To ease the burden of childhood's pain.

#1 WOMAN: Anne Morrow Lindberg views middle age as a time of second flowering. She compares middle age with teen age. She says that the growing pains are the same: discontent, restlessness, doubt, despair and longing. Teenagers accept these as growth signs. Paradoxically, middle-agers accept them as death signs.

#2 WOMAN: May Sarton writes that when a woman has artificial flowers that need dusting twice a year, but never die, she is closing herself off from any understanding of death. But when she has to remain thirty-nine, she is arresting her own growth.

#3 WOMAN: Margaret Mead said she had more energy and felt better after menopause than before. She called this spurt of energy PMZ. Post Menopausal Zest.

CHORUS: *(enthusiastic exclamation)*
    Post Menopausal Zest. WOW!

CHORUS: *(sung to the tune of the Pepsi Cola commercial)*
    PMZ is what we've got
    When you're older it's a lot
    Of fun to have,
    It is the best,
    We call it Post Men-o-pausal Zest.

#4 WOMAN: *(emphatically)* That's all well and good, but I want to know what happens. What does menopause feel like?

The following lines are spoken in rapid succession so that the audience will have a sense of the contradictory nature of the signs of menopause. It is sugested that members of the cast might want to add some of their personal experiences.

#5 WOMAN: I had hot flashes.

#6 WOMAN: I never had a single thing. Nothing.

#1 WOMAN: I cried a lot. My husband called me weepy.

#2 WOMAN: So did mine and I divorced him.

#3 WOMAN: I went back to college and got a degree.

#4 WOMAN: I started a better job.

#5 WOMAN: I became a lesbian.

#6 WOMAN: I saw a feminist therapist and my life improved.

#1 WOMAN: I lost my fear of becoming pregnant.

#2 WOMAN: Just as each girl's menarche is different, so is every woman's menopause.

#3 WOMAN: A woman can have a similar flow less often, or a larger flow regularly.

#4 WOMAN: She may have regular periods until they just stop. Quite suddenly and without warning.

#5 WOMAN: Did you know that statistically only about 10 percent of all women have hot flashes?

CHORUS: *(with anger)*
    Our mothers never told us.

#6 WOMAN: *(very angry)* How could they tell us when they had no knowledge! When all the world around them forced our mothers into silence about the most intimate parts of their female lives!

CHORUS: *(with true rage)*
    When all the world made a profit from our mother's ignorance.

WOMEN #1, #2, #3 TRIO:
    We are the myths of modern medicine
    Advising, always advising
    Listening but hearing little

#4 WOMAN: I am a doctor called Bleary
    I call woman patients "My Dearie"
    I put in my thumb
    And with a cold speculum
    And I think myself clever and cheery.

CHORUS:
    Always advising
    Listening but hearing little.

#5 WOMAN: I am a doctor named Boor
I perform surgery on the poor.
I think there's no use
For an old u-ter-use
When you cannot have kids anymore.

CHORUS:
Advising, always advising
Listening but hearing little.

#6 WOMAN: I am a shrink named Confession
My specialty lies in depression.
I'll pry off the lid
From ego to id
And charge one hundred a session.

CHORUS:
Listening, but hearing little.

#4 WOMAN: I am a doctor named Stealth
Who's built an enormous wealth
By prescribing for ills
Small packets of pills
And capsules and drugs for your health

#2 WOMAN: I tried sleeping pills but after three nights they became less effective, so I just quit. I didn't want to get hooked.

#1 WOMAN: We need to tell the medical profession.

CHORUS: *(Interrupting)*
The worst thing that can happen
When you're up all night
Is that sooner or later
You get tired and go to sleep

#1 WOMAN: *(Sings song to the tune of the Major General's song from Pirates of Penzance - or lines can be recited, reading them as rapidly as possible.)*

I am the very model of a modern pharmaceutical
I've pills and potions
Cures and lotions
Soothing to your cuticle.

I've seltzer pills to make you belch
And pills for regularity
I've drops for cleansing nasal clogs
And drops for bright-eyed clarity.

I've Thorazine to bring you down
And Elavil to take you up —
I've Soma pills for muscles tight
And No-Doze pills to wake you up.

I've Valium for worry warts
And Estrogen for heat control
I've Pheno-barb for wakeful nights
and Ortho pills for birth control

I've fine print information
Which will tell you all the side effects —
Assuming you survive so long
You won't have died of the effect.

For pills and potions
Cures and lotions
Soothing to your cuticle,
I am the very model of a modern pharmaceutical.

#4 WOMAN: I don't want a cure for menopause..

#3 WOMAN: And I don't want a prevention for age.

CHORUS: We will not be tranquilized out of our growth by
packets of pills.

#2 WOMAN: *(In a nasal twang, fast, like a hawker at a circus or*
pace around the stage in a Groucho Marx-type walk.
Whatever you do, ham it up. Have fun with it.)
I am the myth of multi-media.
I shriek at you on television and on radio.
I whisper at you from every corner of the grocery shelf.
I beckon you from all the billboards on the highway.
Do you want to maintain that youthful, sexy, glamorous
feeling you used to have?
Then take 100% American, it's the cure for everything.

OPTIONAL
CHORUS: *All women dance together in a can-can, shuffle, jig,*
whatever they most enjoy. They should be as slapstick as they
want. While dancing they sing.

Tr-ra-ra BOOM Ti-Ay
Tr-ra-ra BOOM Ti-Ay
Tr-ra-ra BOOM Ti-Ay
Tr-ra-ra BOOM Ti-Ay

#5 WOMAN: I sell you jeans, I sell you youth
I sell you lies, I call it truth.
TV ads are what I do,
Listen here while I show you.

(Sings in a coy falsetto to tune of 'Wash that Man Right Out of My
Hair'' - from South Pacific).

I'm gonna wash that grey right outta my hair
I'm gonna wash that grey right outta my hair
With Living Dare shampoo.

OPTIONAL
CHORUS:
    Tr-ra-ra BOOM Ti-Ay
    Tr-ra-ra BOOM Ti-Ay
    Tr-ra-ra BOOM Ti-Ay
    Tr-ra-ra BOOM Ti-Ay

#6 WOMAN: I'm the guy from the radio
    I do that talk and music show
    Sponsors pay to brainwash you
    Here's the stuff we like to do.

(Reads in a husky, somewhat oily voice)

You probably thought your age would never catch up with you.
 Unfortunately, it has.
If you smooth   Oil of Okay on your face and throat every night,
It will replace those tell-tale age lines
With soft, smooth, unwrinkled skin.
No woman wants to feel older than she is.
Oil of Okay can help you feel younger.
Be Okay.
Get Oil of Okay, today.

 OPTIONAL:
 CHORUS:
    Tr-ra-ra BOOM Ti-Ay
    Tr-ra-ra BOOM Ti-Ay
    Tr-ra-ra BOOM Ti-Ay
    Tr-ra-ra BOOM Ti-Ay

Duet: #3 AND #4 WOMEN:
We are the tools that ad men use.
    Words and Symbols that they choose

#3 WOMAN: *(Interrupts trio with her pronouncement.)*
 I am sex and he is youth
 We use words to give our proof.

#4 WOMAN: We give you ten thousand messages every day of your life.

#1 WOMAN: He bombards you with buying.

#2 WOMAN: He pressures you with products.

DUET: We're sex and we're youth
We're youth and we're sex
You cannot escape us.

#4 WOMAN *(A sing-song voice in sugary tones)*
Listen - listen to my words:
You look so young.
You don't look your age.
You don't act your age.

(Returns to normal voice)

I say 'young' when I mean energetic.
I say 'young' when I mean alert.
I say 'young' when I mean lively.
I teach you words to say.
I'm youth and he's sex.

#3 WOMAN: Listen.
Listen to my words.
I say 'sexy' when I mean affectionate.
I say 'sexy' when I mean caring.
I say 'sexy' when I mean sensuous.
I teach you words to say.
I'm sex and he's youth.
We are the identical, diabolical twins.
We teach. . .

#1 WOMAN: *(interrupts in a firm angry voice.)*
Hey, knock it off.
You've strangled us with words of hate long enough.

#2 WOMAN: Listen.
　　　　Listen to these words.
　　　　Magic varied words from a to z,
　　　　From Aleph to Tav,
　　　　From Ardent to Zestful.

(Entire cast speaks the following words. They are spoken with a burst, not a shout, of emphasis and joyful enthusiasm. They are voiced very quickly, one after another. The sounds of the words should make happy explosions as if many ping-pong balls were bouncing in the air.

Ardent	Able	Amorous
Attractive	Assertive	Brilliant
Brave	Caring	Centered
Compassionate	Calm	Curious
Creative	Careful	Dependable
Determined	Efficient	Energetic
Enthusiastic	Fair	Friendly
Gentle	Humorous	Happy
Independent	Intelligent	Intuitive
Jovial	Joyful	Loyal
Loving	Nurturing	Outgoing
Perceptive	Reliable	Resourceful
Strong	Self-sufficient	Sensual
Supportive	Talented	Thoughful
Warm	Witty	Zestful

CHORUS: Sisters
　　　　Let us gather together in small groups
　　　　And in large.
　　　　Let us welcome middle age and menopause
　　　　With knowledge and without fear.

#6 WOMAN: Anthropologist Margaret Mead tells us that the human female is the only female in the animal kingdom who undergoes the process of menopause. All other female animals remain fertile, producing offspring until their death.

#4 WOMAN: Menopause is nature's way of giving each woman time within her lifetime to explore her talents, develop her skills and fulfill her desires. Now free from the fear of pregnancy. Now free from pins, pads, belts, and tampons. Now released from the responsibility of childrearing.

CHORUS: We must carry our wisdom out into the world
　　As we carried our infants.

RIGHTS OF PASSAGE

Section Three—THE AGES OF WOMAN

This section, in poetry, can be read by each woman in the cast becoming one of the ages. It can also be read, side stage, by one woman, while another woman plays a quiet instrument such as a lute, dulcimer, guitar, or recorder for background. It may be performed in dance, with the voice of one or several women as background while other women dance the ages of woman.

#3 WOMAN:

INFANT:

> I am the infant small
> and frightened.
> I am the baby
> hungry and cold.
> I cry.
> I cry, Mama.
> Hold me, woman.
> Feed me from your body.
> Nourish me, Mother,
> So that I may grow into womanhood.
>
> I am the baby
> Hungry and wet.
> I cry.
> I cry, hold me.
> Dry me.
> Love me.
>
> I am growing into you,
> Woman.

#4 WOMAN:

CHILD:

I am the child
bright-eyed and believing.
I see fairies
living in the honeysuckle.
I bounce with laughter.
I hide from the world in my sandhole.
Find me!
Find me!
I see you!

I am the child
who won't stay still when you, woman,
braid my long curls.
I am the child
screaming,
crying -
understand me!
Please hear what I say.
Love me.
I am the child, trying to believe.
I am growing into you,
Woman.

#5 WOMAN:

GIRL:

I am the girl
flying and reaching.
I am the girl
sailing down the road on my bicycle.
I am the girl
sullen and sure
kicking a rock in the road.
I am the girl
reading my lessons
writing my papers
struggling to please.

I am the girl
watching.

Watching
my chest is growing two bumps.
Two bumps into breasts.
I am the girl.
I look into the mirror.
Who are you? I ask.

I am the girl
growing into you,
Woman.

#6 WOMAN:

TEENAGE WOMAN

I am the teen age woman
As new and as fresh
as a brook in Springtime.
My breasts are ice-cream cones,
Delicious.
I pose before the mirror
I tilt my head this way
I tilt my hips that way
I examine the fuzz that marks my crotch.
I turn round,
Here I am too small
And here I am too big.
Oh, I wish I were different,
But alas I am not.

I am growing into you,
Woman.

#1 WOMAN:

YOUNG WOMAN:

I am the young woman
Not doing much of anything with my life.
Pick up a job here and there,
never been married.
I have some lovers,
they come and go,
I often think my next lover
will be THE one.

I am the young woman,
Seeking.
I am a thistledown.
Roving, traveling, studying,
Tasting new places,
Meeting new ideas,
Stretching my mind.
Shaping myself.

I am growing into you,
Woman.

#2 WOMAN:

WOMAN DOMESTICATED:

I am woman,
Domesticated, but not tamed.
All day long I hear voices:
Mother-do-this, Mother do-that,
Dear-come-here, Dear-go-away.
Will-you, won't-you
Can-you, can't-you. . .
STOP.
Please, stop.
Sometimes, there is no me,
Only voices.

I am the woman,
Wifing, mothering, nurturing,
Every night, when small arms
Reach round my neck,
Sing me a song, Mommie,
I turn into a lullaby.
I am needed.
I am loved.

I am growing into you,
Woman.

#3 WOMAN:

WORKING WOMAN :

> I am woman,
> Working,
> Loving my work,
> Loving myself as I work.
> Sometimes it's tedious,
> But once in a while,
> When I say or do something
>   that makes a real difference,
> I am pleased.
> I know who I am.
>
> I am growing into you,
> Woman.

#4 WOMAN:

LOVERS:

I am the woman, a lover,
My breasts are ripe.
My lover holds them.
We laugh.
Our legs entwine like wild grape vines,
    growing in the forest.
Flying,
    we reach for other worlds.

I am growing into you,
Woman.

#5 WOMAN:

MID-LIFE WOMAN:

I am the mid-life woman,
    like a Chinese bronze with patina.
I look into the mirror;
    a wrinkle here, a crinkle there.
I tilt my hips this way
I tilt my head that way.
Here I am too small,
There I am too big.
Oh, I wish I were different
But alas I am not.

I am the woman
Like vintage wine
Like Indian summer,
My own center of gravity.

I am mid-life woman,
A garden in second bloom.

#6 WOMAN:

CRONE:

I am the woman,
old.
You may call me
Crone
Wise one.
Grand-Mother.
If you look, you can see
all that has gone before me
Is written on my face.

Ask me my life,
If you listen,
I will tell you my wisdom.

I am woman,
Old.
I have been all that you are:
I am infant
child,
girl,
teenage woman,
wife,
mother, mid-life woman.

I am working
I am loving.
All of these things I am.
Moving.
Changing.
Living.

Woman -
You are becoming me.

Section Four—THE RITUAL

The entire cast gathers around the candlelit table, forming a semi-circle. They assemble with a combination of solemnity and joy, seriousness and gaiety. They gather to make a ceremony celebrating and glorifying an important passage in their lives. They touch the shoulder of the woman to their right.

(*touch shoulder of woman to the right*)

#1. WOMAN: We, women of all ages
Gather together within our circle.
Our hands touch, we bind together
The secrets of our womanhood - our oneness in sisterhood,
Our sacred pact with our Mothers:
Earth,
Moon
and Sea.

#2. WOMAN: We gather in the name of all women
Of all time,
Celebrating our passage
Into a new world.

#3 WOMAN:

This ritual takes place
in an ordinary room
which can be anywhere.

CHORUS:

We gather in our room
To celebrate the fruits
Of one season of our lives.

The Women stand apart. A bowl or basket of red flowers is passed around among the women in the semi-circle. Each woman takes several flowers. As she reads her lines, she gently tosses a flower, or several flowers, into the audience.

#2 WOMAN:

This flower is the menstrual blood of all women. The only blood which flows with never an injury. *(throws flower)*

#3 WOMAN:
This flower is the blood of my menses which no longer comes to me. *(throws flower)*

#4 WOMAN:
This flower is the blood of the full moon, rising in greeting to our Mother Earth. *(throws flower)*

#5 WOMAN:
This flower is the blood of childbirth, bearing the miracle of life, the wonders of love, and the joy of hope. *(throws flower)*

#6 WOMAN:
This flower is the blood of our lives as we have lived them, one drop at a time. Wear the blood gently, sisters. Let it penetrate your life and permeate your days. *(throws flower)*

CHORUS:

We gather in the name of all women
Of all time,
Celebrating our passage
Into a new world.

#2, 3, & 4 WOMEN:

We sing of life and love,
Of children and illness.

#1, 5, & 6 WOMEN:

We sing of death.
Mourning and weeping.

CHORUS (entire cast):

We sing of all the days of our lives.
We sing of all the days yet to become.

Any remaining flowers are thrown into the audience.

#1 WOMAN: I'll tell you how a rose is cold
When you take it in your hand,
And where the small san dollar lives
Along the ocean strand.

I'll show you where the whippoorwill
Hides her song at break of day,
And how sisters loving sisters,
Can fade your fears away.

Reprise of the last verses of "Militant Menopausal Woman" is optional. When the performance ends with "We sing of all the days. . . " Rights of Passage gives both audience and performers a serious and a spiritual impact at closing. If the performers want to end on a lighter note, a singer, chanter should repeat, as shown, the verses from the song "Militant Menopausal Woman". She should lead the cast in hand clapping and invite the audience to join in singing. Entire cast should exit to the hand claps of the audience.

(Option: Invite audience to clap and chant along)

> Because, y'see
> I'm a militant menopausal woman
> A worker, a lover, and a wife.
> I'm a militant menopausal woman,
> Making myself a new life.
>
> Oh yeah,
> Making myself a new life.

(Audience and chorus repeat as long as feels comfortable.)

Optional Ending:

#6 WOMAN:

> I'll tell you how a rose is cold
> When you take it in your hand,
> And where the small sand dollar lives
> Along the sandy strand.
>
> I'll show you where the whippoorwill
> Hides her song at break of day.
> And how sisters loving sisters,
> Can fade your cares away.

PART VIII

SONG

Coming Home

Bearing words born new unto each day
Speaking bold where only silence lay
As we dare to rise and lead the way
We're coming home, we're coming home

As the full moon waxes into wane
Changing, yielding all that she did gain
As from death she dares be born again
We're coming home, we're coming home

To reclaim the thinking of our minds
Leaving shackles lying far behind
Bearing hope for every soul confined
We're coming home, we're coming home

To create a world of joy and peace
Where the power of justice does release
Love abounding, wars forever cease
We're coming home, we're coming home

PART IX

LETTER

The following is a letter written by Nadine Stair at age 85:

IF I HAD MY LIFE TO LIVE OVER

If I had my life to live over, I'd dare to make more mistakes next time. I'd relax; I'd limber up. I would be sillier than I have been this trip. I would take fewer things seriously. I would take more chances. I would climb more mountains and swim more rivers. I would eat more ice cream and less beans. I would perhaps have more actual troubles, but I'd have fewer imaginary ones.

You see, I'm one of those people who live sensibly and sanely hour after hour, day after day. Oh, I've had my moments, and if I had it to do over again, I'd have more of them. In fact, I'd try to have nothing else. Just moments, one after the other, instead of living so many years ahead of each day. I've been one of those persons who never goes anywhere without a thermometer, a hot water bottle, a raincoat and a parachute. If I had it to do over again, I would travel lighter than I have.

If I had my life to live over again, I would start barefoot earlier in the spring and stay that way later in the fall. I would go to more dances; I would ride more merry-go-rounds. I would pick more daisies.

Louisville, KY

"Gardener"
Each month the blood sheets down like good red rain.
   I am the gardener
Nothing grows without me.

Half-lives Erica Jong, 1973

                    I was as you say born under the moon
and my belly-lining plays a ritual imitation of that lunar
dissonance.

—Pamela Victorine.

from *Menses: A Seasonal*

In man, the shedding of blood is always associated with injury,
disease or death. Only the female half of humanity was seen to have
the magical ability to bleed profusely and still rise phoenix-like each
month from the gore.

—Estelle R. Ramey

PART X

READING

"LET'S CELEBRATE MIDDLE-AGE"

And so we celebrate middle-age.

If you are over 50, or near 50, I want you to take your right arm, that's right, put your right hand out in front of you. Now, reach over your left shoulder. . . that's right, and give yourself a pat on the back. Good.

You made it! You're lucky to be alive! Enjoy your life! Respect yourself! Celebrate middle-age and your (male or) female. . . menopause. Consider it a "right" of passage. This is the time:
TO GROW
TO CHANGE
TO BE FREE
TO COME HOME TO THE SPIRIT IN YOUR SOUL
TO CREATE A WORLD OF PEACE AND JOY
     WITH LOVE ABOUNDING. . .
TO BE YOURSELF
TO ENJOY YOURSELF
TO LOVE YOURSELF

Now, I believe that everyone needs a minimum of four hugs a day. Twelve are better.

As we end our program, I invite all of you to extend your arms and be sure that you get at least four hugs before leaving this building (sanctuary, room, church. . .) .

This is a lovely day.

How good it is to be alive and to be with friends.

Thank you for celebrating middle-age and menopause with us— ✳

FIFTY—NOT FIFTEEN
IS THE HEYDAY OF A WOMAN'S LIFE

Then the forces hitherto finding an outlet in flirtations, courtship, conjugal and maternal love, are garnered in the brain to find expression in intellectual achievements, in spiritual friendships and beautiful thoughts, in music, poetry, and art. The young have no memories with which to build their lives, none of the pleasures of retrospection. Neither has youth a monopoly of the illusions of hope, for that is eternal; to the end we have something still to hope. And here age has the advantage of basing its hopes on something rational and attainable. From experience we understand the situation, we have knowledge of human nature, we learn how to control ourselves, to treat children with tenderness, servants with consideration, and our equals with proper respect. Years bring wisdom and charity; pity rather than criticism; sympathy, rather than condemnation.

Elizabeth Cady Stanton

ELIZABETH CADY STANTON

"Every form of religion which has breathed upon this earth has degraded woman. Man himself could not do this; but when he declares, 'Thus saith the Lord,' of course he can do it."

—Elizabeth Cady Stanton
(1815-1902)

SELECTED BIBLIOGRAPHY

Anderson, Mary. **The Menopause**, Faber & Faber, 1983

Boston Women's Health Book Collection. **Our Bodies, Ourselves**, 2nd ed, Simon & Schuster, 1979. (Excellent general book for women about their bodies.)

Burnett, Raymond. **Menopause: All Your Questions Answered**, Contemporary Books, 1987.

Clausen Muriel C. **Menopause: Vitamins & You**, M.C. Clausen, 1980

Clay, Vidal S. **Women: Menopause and Middle Age**, Know, Inc., 1977 *(Information on Estrogen Replacement Therapy)*

Coope, Jean. **The Menopause**, Arco 1984.

Davis, M. Edward & Dona Meilach. **Doctor Discusses Menopause & Estrogens**, Budlong, 1987.

Delaney, Janice, Mary Jane Lupton and Emily Toth. **The Curse: A Cultural History of Menstruation**, New American Library, 1977

Downing, Christine. **Journey Through Menopause: A Personal Rite of Passage**, Crossroad, New York, 1987.

Fairlie, Judy, et al. **Menopause: A Time for Positive Change**, Blandford Press, England, 1987.

Gannon, Linda R. **Menstrual Disorders & Menopause: Etiology, Maintenance & Treatment**, Prager, 1985.

Gosden, R.C. **Biology of Menopause: The Casues & Consequences of Ovarian Aging**, Acadamic Press, 1985.

Greene, John G. **The Social & Psychological Origins of the Climateric Syndrome**, Gower Publishing Co., 1984.

Greenwood, Sadja. **Menopause, Naturally: Preparing for the Second Half of Life**, Volcano Press, 1984.

LeShan, Eda. **The Wonderful Crisis of Middle Age**, Warner Books, 1974.

Millette, Brenda & Joellen Hawkins. **The Passage Trough Menopause: Women's Life in Transition**, Reston 1983.

————. **Women & The Menopause: A Book for & about Women & the Climateric**, Reston, 1983.

Ojeda, Linda. **Menopause Without Medicine**, Borgo Press, 1987.

O'Neill, Daniel J. **Menopause & It's Effect on the Family**, United Press of America, 1982.

Quinava, Ruby M. **Menopause: Medical Research & Reference Guidebook**, ABBE Pubs Assn, 1985.

Reitz, Rosetta. **Menopause, A Positive Approach**, Penguin Books, 1977. *(Easy to read, informative on sex, aging, nutrition, estogen, and more.)*

Rose, Luisa, ed. **The Menopause Book**. *(Doctors give medical answeres to questions affecting middle aged women. Helpful section on sex.)*

Rogers, Natalie. **Emerging Woman**, Personal Point Press, P.O.Box 789, Point Reyes Station, CA 94956. *(Personal account of one woman's divorce and transition to a new life.)*

Rubin, Lillian. **Woman of a Certain Age**, Harper & Row, New York, 1979. *(Excellent sociological study of middle class mid-life women.)*

Sarton, May. **Journal of a Solitude**, W.W. Norton, New York, 1983.

Science of Life Books Editorial Committee. **Woman's Change of Life**, Thorsons Publishers, 1983.

Seaman, Barbara and G. Seaman, M.D. **Women and the Crisis in Sex Hormones**, Bantam Books, New York, 1978.

Sheehy, Gail. **Passages**, Bantam Books, New York, 1977.

Tengbom, Mildred. **September Morning: A Practical Guide for the Middle Years**, Brethen, 1985.

Trien, Susan. **Change of Life: The Menopause Handbook**, Fawcett, 1986.

Voda, Ann M., et al, eds. **Changing Perspectives on Menopause**, U of Texas Press, 1982.

Weideger, Paula. **Menstruation and Menopause: The Physiology, the Psychology, the Myth and the Reality**, Afred A. Knopf, Inc., New York, 1976.

SENECA FALLS
-1848-

SENECA FALLS - 1848

TABLE OF CONTENTS

WHAT IT TOOK TO WIN SUFFRAGE

Fifty-two years of campaigning; 56 referenda to male voters; 480 efforts to get state legislatures to submit suffrage amendments; 277 campaigns to get state party conventions to include women's suffrage planks; 47 campaigns to get state constitutional conventions to write women's suffrage into state constitutions; 30 campaigns to get Presidential party conventions to adopt women's suffrage planks into party platforms; and 19 successive campaigns with 19 successive Congresses.

It took 72 consecutive years of struggle for women to get the vote in the United States.

When women won the right to vote in England, men could vote at age 21; women not until they were 30.

There are still a number of nations which prohibit women from voting.

Lucy
Stone

Susan B. Anthony
at the age of 48

Martha
Wright

Antoinette
Brown

Mary Ann
McClintock

Most women in the "first wave of feminism" did not question the patriarchal family structure. They wanted education, change in the marriage laws, birth control, the right to vote.

Lucy Stone

*Elizabeth
Cady Stanton
and her son
Henry in 1854*

*James and
Lucretia Mott,
about 1842*

Joining the others in composing resolutions and speeches was:
  Elizabeth W. McClintock

*

As Stanton would later tell the story, "These four ladies, sitting round the tea-table of Richard Hunt, a prominent Friend near Waterloo, decided to put their long-talked-of resolution into action, and before the twilight deepened into night, the call was written, and sent to the *Seneca County Courier.* On Sunday morning they met in Mrs. McClintock's parlor to write their declaration, resolutions, and to consider subjects for speeches. As the convention was to assemble in **three** days, the time was short for such productions; but having no experience in the *modus operandi of getting up conventions, nor in that kind of literature, they were quite innocent of the herculean labors they proposed. . . "*

The Seneca Falls "Declaration" is without a doubt the most famous document produced by the women's movement in the United States. It marks the birth, not of feminist thinking, but of the feminist movement in the United States. It has stood as a model for countless subsequent declarations on women's rights.

Lucretia Mott

> *A woman is nobody. A wife is everything. A pretty girl is equal to ten thousand men , and a mother is, next to God, all powerful. . . the ladies of Philadelphia, therefore, are resolved to maintain their rights as Wives, Bells, Virgins, and Mothers and not as Women.*
>
> *-Philadelphia* **Public Ledger and Daily Transcript 1848**

"A Woman is Nobody"

The *Ledger's* editorial was a response to the Seneca Falls "Declaration of Sentiments." Millions of words have been written on women's rights since, but nowhere is the basic opposition to equality stated so plainly: "A woman is nobody."

Men were saying that a woman is "somebody" only when playing the role of belle, virgin, wife or mother. From the outset of the women's movement, feminists have rejected this type of thinking and have struggled for the right to be *somebody* in their own right rather than merely an appendage of their father or husband. A "woman", an adult female person, wants to live her own life rather than fulfill expectations of what a man wants —as a "belle" a woman finds herself looking into mirrors asking if she is really pretty. As a "wife" she becomes a servant to a man and a house and sometimes plays the role of putting her husband's wealth on display. As "mother" she lives for her offspring instead of herself.

A key tactic to keep women in traditional roles and out of positions of power has been the cultural message that women could only find fulfillment as belles, wives, and mothers. Women have been told in sermons, magazines, articles, movie scripts, advertising copy, song lyrics, and newspaper editorials—at home and at school—that they had to choose between career and family. Men need not choose between fatherhood and career.

What must change if women are to have lives of their own? How can we translate the vision of Elizabeth Cady Stanton, Lucretia Mott and our other brave foremothers into reality?

The first women's rights convention was held July 19th and 20th, 1848 in Seneca Falls, New York. For historical perspective, 1848 was the year the U.S. treaty with Britain set the Oregon territory at the 49th parallel, and 1848 was the year the war with Mexico ended giving the United States, California, Nevada, Utah, New Mexico and Texas. Europe was in turmoil with the 1848 revolutions. San Francisco's population was about 800, but the California Gold Rush would explode in a few months and within two years that number would jump to over 30,000. The Civil War was thirteen years in the future.

The United States was 62 years old and, under English Common Law, married women had **no** rights. None. Zero. Her various appellations: "Lady", "Wife", "Belle", "Virgin" and "Mother" all spoke to her value as seen through the eyes of a man - her protector and sovereign.

When the brilliant Elizabeth Cady Stanton (1815-1902) married Henry Stanton in 1840 they honeymooned in London in order to attend the World Anti-Slavery Convention. It was here that Elizabeth met Lucretia Mott (1793-1880), a Quaker and an abolitionist who aided escaped slaves through the Underground Railroad. Lucretia, a good public speaker, was an authorized delegate to the Convention.

Elizabeth and Lucretia quickly became friends over their shared **outrage** when women were denied the right to participate in the World Anti-Slavery Convention. They met at every opportunity and vowed to form a society for **women's** rights when they returned to America. On one occasion Elizabeth went to hear Lucretia preach in a Unitarian church; it was the first time she had heard a woman speak in public.

Although the two women corresponded, they did not meet again until July, 1848 when Jane Hunt of Waterloo, New York invited Elizabeth Cady Stanton, Lucretia Mott and Lucretia's sister, Martha C. Wright, and Mary Ann McClintock to a meeting in her home.

---

*These **Background Notes** may be read to introduce the **Dramatic Reading.**

The popular way to address social problems in those days was to call a meeting and list grievances. Over tea, these five women planned the first woman's rights conference. Using the Declaration of Independence as a framework, they were in accord with their twelve grievances and demands, except for Stanton's radical 9th Resolution: "RESOLVED: It is the duty of women of this country to secure to themselves their sacred right to the elected franchise."

Women vote? Don't be absurd! Everyone knew women's brains were too soft for hard politics. 'Woman's sphere" was the home. But this was a time of social change. Women, especially Quaker women active in the temperance and anti-slavery movements, were speaking out in public. They were becoming uppity!

With only a few days to plan the conference, they met at Jane Hunt's home and then at Elizabeth McClintock's home. When July 19th arrived, the roads to the Conference were jammed with carriages and carts; some had come from 50 miles away. They did **not** expect the large turnout of 40 men and 240 women to the first day of the conference (men weren't invited but were allowed to participate*).

After the conference, they did **not** expect the virulent hostility heaped upon them by men of the press and the pulpit.

They did **not** expect it would take 72 years for women to get the vote.

They did **not** expect that at the end of the Twentieth Century—today—women would **still** be persuading their Sisters to stop thinking of themselves as genteel ladies and get down to serious business as citizens, women, and people.

Whenever possible, the dialogue in **Seneca Falls - 1848** is taken from direct quotes so some of the language syntax may sound stilted. With dramatic license, this is historical fiction and I wish to acknowledge the late Mrs. E.M. Bailey for her ideas used in this dramatic reading (circa 1948; see **Response** 10/85).

Meg Bowman
San Jose, CA

*It was called a 'promiscuous' audience when both men and women were present.

CAST

1. MARY ANN WILSON McCLINTOCK:
(Mrs. Thomas McClintock) Quaker who lives modestly in Waterloo, N.Y., located 6 miles north of Seneca Falls. She, her husband and two of her daughters, Mary Ann and Elizabeth, attend the Seneca Falls convention. She wears the Quaker bonnet.

2. MARTHA COFFIN WRIGHT:
(Mrs. David Wright) At age 42, she is 13 years younger than her sister, Lucretia Mott. Houseguest from Auburn, New York, Martha, wife and mother of seven, is a knitter and a doer. Susan B. Anthony called her "clear sighted, true and steadfast almost beyond all other women." Known for her warmth and humor, she has a 'lighter tone' than Lurectia and is not a Quaker, having married out of the Society of Friends. Like Stanton, she has little regard for organized religion and supported women's sufferage immediately.

3. JANE MASTEN HUNT:
(Mrs. Richard Hunt) She is the fourth wife of a wealthy Quaker farmer, mother of three and step-mother to three more children. The action takes place in her lovely home just outside of Waterloo, New York.

4. LUCRETIA COFFIN MOTT:
(Mrs. James Mott) Abolitionist and a good public speaker from Philadelphia, PA. At age 55, she is slender and of extraordinary composure and intelligence. Lucretia has a high forehead and straight brown hair. She wears the simple grey and white Quaker dress and the light, gathered cap she always wore.

5. ELIZABETH CADY STANTON:
(Mrs. Henry Stanton) In 1848 she is 32 and mother of three sons (6, 4, 2). Because of her politically active husband's failing health, they have recently moved from Boston to Seneca Falls, a city with a population of 4,000 in upstate New York. Scholar and leader, she became an eloquent speaker and devoted her life to women's rights. She has the lead role.

6. ANTOINETTE L. BROWN:

Scholar, 23, working for equal rights with Lucy Stone at Oberlin College. She later became the first woman to be ordained minister in the U.S. and married Samuel Blackwell (brother to Lucy Stone's husband, Henry). Not a Quaker.

7. ELIZABETH W. McCLINTOCK:

Daughter to Mary Ann McClintock, age 27. The second planning meeting was held in her home on Sunday, July 16th. She was later appointed secretary to the first woman's right organization. She wears the Quaker bonnet.

8. EMILY PETERSON:

Quaker from Waterloo, New York.

9. SALLY BRIDGES*:

Widow who supports five children by doing laundry. She has only one speaking part.

One woman can play the role of SALLY BRIDGES and ANTOINETTE BROWN, or ELIZABETH McCLINTOCK, or EMILY PETERSON.

SETTING:

Parlor of Jane Hunt's home near Waterloo, New York, Thursday, July 13, 1848. The parlor contains elegant furniture of that period, including three chairs, a small sofa and a tea table. The action occupies a part of one mid-summer day; tea is served.

Elizabeth Cady Stanton & Son

PRODUCTION NOTES:

Seneca Falls - 1848 - can be presented as - :

1) a one-act play of three scenes with the cast memorizing their parts.
2) a dramatic reading with the cast reading the script, **or**
3) a combination with the PROLOGUE and POSTSCRIPT read and most of the DRAMA script memorized.

When presented as a **dramatic reading,** caution the cast to look at the person who is reading, and **not** down at their script. The cast should have at least one read-through before their performance.

As the Hunts were wealthy, you may provide an elaborate parlor setting of the period, or merely place three chairs and a small sofa on the stage area plus a small table and tea service.

Women dressed in long skirts, bonnets and light shawls of the 1840's will provide an aura of that time.

When one woman plays SALLY BRIDGES and ELIZABETH McCLINTOCK, ANTOINETTE BROWN or EMILY PETERSON, a quick costume change will be required for her to "become" SALLY BRIDGES. She may remove her bonnet, tousle her hair, and put on a large working class apron.

PROPS:

3 chairs and a small divan/or sofa.
1 small table with tea service for two or three.
If desired: A desk for MARY ANN McCLINTOCK to write on.

Backdrop can include exit RT to another room off from the parlor, and exit LFT via a "front door" with a "window" looking out to the front yard.

MARY ANN McCLINTOCK has a writing pad and pen either in her bag, or placed on the tea table.

MARTHA WRIGHT knits throughout the play.

LUCRETIA MOTT, MARY ANN McCLINTOCK, ELIZABETH W. McCLINTOCK, JANE HUNT and EMILY PETERSON are dressed in traditional Quaker attire; plain grey or black long skirts with simple design blouses and plain gathered bonnets.
These 5 grey or white bonnets or caps will probably have to be made; they are essential to give an aura of authenticity.

SALLY BRIDGES, a laundress, is dressed as a working class woman. She can wear a large apron.

ELIZABETH CADY STANTON, MARTHA C. WRIGHT and ANTOINETTE BROWN are dressed in upper-middle-class 1848 fashion—long skirts, bonnets and light summer shawls. If STANTON wears a shawl, you may wish to provide a table or chair for the hostess, JANE HUNT, to place it on when STANTON enters.

ANTOINETTE BROWN, ELIZABETH McCLINTOCK and EMILY PETERSON could wear gloves.

STAGE SETTING AND PLACES:

Part II   Drama

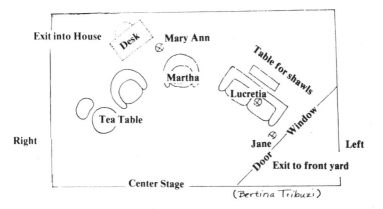

(Bertina Tribuzi)

NOTE: When this dramatic reading **Seneca Falls - 1848** is used as part of a program (e.g., Women's History Week Program, N.O.W. meeting, or a church service. . .), four members of the cast (MARY ANN, MARTHA, JANE and LUCRETIA) sit off-stage RT, and four members of the cast (ELIZABETH STANTON, ELIZA-BETH McCLINTOCK, ANTOINETTE and EMILY) sit off-stage LFT.

Number of Speaking Parts per Reader:

Performer	Part I	Part II	Part III
Elizabeth Cady Stanton	0	27	0
Jane Hunt	2	15	0
Lucretia Mott	1	15	0
Mary Ann McClintock	2	11	0
Martha C. Wright	2	10	0
Antoinette Brown	0	0	4
Emily Peterson	0	0	4
Elizabeth McClintock	0	0	5
Sally Bridges	1	0	0

How To Make The Quaker Bonnets:

1. Using an old white sheet, draw a 15" to 18" diameter circle.

2. Cut it out, turn up 1/4" and stitch for a smooth edge.

3. Measure 4" from the edge and using basting stitches make three separate concentric circles about 1/4" apart toward the crown. Be sure to start and end at the same point for each circle of stitching.

4. Gather to fit the crown and tie the basting threads.

5. Distribute gathers evenly (pin in place).

6. Stitch gathers at least twice (small straight machine stitch).

7. Use bias tape to further secure and cover gathered rows of stitches.

8. Fold outer stitched edge up to meet the gathers to make a brim. The stitched edge must be gathered and sewn to the stitched crown. (Use gathering stitch, or bias tape as trim; or sew by hand).

These "Quaker bonnets" appear as "poofs on the head" and resemble English dust caps. They are worn by Lucretia Mott, Jane Hunt, Elizabeth McClintock, Mary Ann McClintock, and either Sally Bridges or Emily Peterson.

You will need five bonnets.

Lucretia Mott

Example of a program:

SENECA FALLS - 1848

A play about the first woman's rights convention.

TIME: A July afternoon - 1848

PLACE: Parlor, Jane Hunt's home,
Waterloo, New York

CAST:

Mary Ann McClintock
Quaker from Waterloo, NY..................................

Martha C. Wright
Sister to Lucretia Mott,
houseguest from Auburn, NY..............................

Jane Hunt
Quaker; hostess..

Lucretia Mott
Quaker, Abolitionist and leader
in Underground Railroad; houeguest from
Philadelphia, PA...

Elizabeth Cady Stanton
Scholar and leader from
Seneca Falls, NY...

Elizabeth W. McClitock
Daughter of Mary Ann McClintock ....

Antoinette Brown
Scholar who worked for equal rights with
Lucy Stone at Oberlin College.............................

Emily Peterson
Quaker from Waterloo, NY..................................

Sally Bridges
Widow who supports 5 children by
doing laundry..

PART I: PROLOGUE
Mary Ann McClintock, Martha Wright, Jane Hunt
and Lucretia Mott set the scene.

PART II: DRAMA
Women plan the first woman's rights convention.

PART III: POSTSCRIPT
Elizabeth W. McClintock, Antoinette Brown and
Emily Peterson tell about the convention.

Why Women's History?

National Women's History Week* sets aside special time each March for schools, communities, organizations, churches and workplaces to recognize and celebrate the lives of countless women.

Women of all races, ages, cultures, ethnic traditions and ways of life are honored for contributing to our shared history - whether in ways grandly eloquent or steadfastly ordinary.

Knowing the true stories of these women's accomplishments can inspire each of us to become more optimistic as we effect change in the long and varied struggle for equal rights.

It is our shared commitment to Women's History and to National Women's History Week that we bring you this program today (this morning/evening. . .).

National Women's History Week always includes International Women's Day, March 8th, a day proclaimed at the turn of the century to recognize the outstanding work of women in the labor movement.

Example of a program:

WOMEN'S HISTORY WEEK PROGRAM

Sunday, March 9

FIRST UNITARIAN CHURCH

San Jose, California

WORLD PREMIER

Dramatic Reading

SENECA FALLS—1848

by

Meg Bowman, Ph.D.

WOMEN'S   HISTORY   WEEK   PROGRAM

Welcome............................... Florance Thompson

Kindling the Chalice .... Children

Announcements.......................... Florance Thompson

Offering........................ "Songs of the Suffragettes",
Elizabeth Knight*

Womens's History Week .... Charlotte Suskind

*Songs of the Suffragettes," Elizabeth Knight. Folkways Records #FH5281

Responsive Reading:
Let Us Now Praise Famous Women . . . . Florance Thompson

Quote:
Philadelphia Public Ledger and Daily Transcript, 1848. . . . . Bob
Ri·chardson

Background Information. . . . . Meg Bowman

Dramatic Reading:
SENECA FALLS—1848
Cast:

Mary Ann McClintock. . . . . Jody Calvert
Martha Wright. . . . . Charlotte Suskind
Jane Hunt . . . . Barbara Van Mourik
Lucretia Mott . . . . Nancy Jones
Elizabeth Cady Stanton . . . . Kathy Kemp
Elizabeth McClintock . . . . Faith Sandberg
Antoinette Brown. . . . . Meg Bowman
Emily Peterson . . . . Evelyn Sheridan
Sally Bridges . . . . Evelyn Sheridan

Time: A July afternoon—1848
Place: Parlor, Jane Hunt's home, Waterloo, NY

PART I: PROLOGUE
    Mary Ann McClintock, Martha Wright, Jane Hunt and
Lucretia Mott set the scene.

PART II: DRAMA
    Women plan the first women's rights convention.

PART III: POSTSCRIPT
    Elizabeth W. McClintock, Antoinette Brown, and
    Emily Peterson tell about the convention.

Song: "Coming Home" . . . . Lindi Ramsden
Closing:. . . . . Lindi Ramdsden

LET US NOW PRAISE FAMOUS WOMEN

Let us now praise famous women
Our foremothers who paved the way—

    THOSE WHO INITIATED CHANGE
    THOSE WHO LOVED JUSTICE
    THOSE WHO MADE THE WORLD GO.

Let us now praise famous women
Those wise and eloquent teachers
Who steadfastly passed on their culture—

    THEIR NURTURING
    THEIR HEALING
    THEIR COUNSEL
    THEIR WISDOM.

Let us now praise famous women
Few were honored in their generation—

    BUT THEY LEFT THEIR NAMES BEHIND THEM
    FOR US TO SING THEIR PRAISES.

Let us now sing praises to—

SUSAN B. ANTHONY, ELIZABETH CADY STANTON,
ALICE PAUL, MARGARET SANGER, EMMA GOLDMAN.

SOJOURNER TRUTH, MARY WOLLSTONECRAFT,
LUCRETIA MOTT, DOROTHEA DIX, HARRIET TUBMAN.

But most of our foremothers are forgotten—

> THEY HAVE NO MEMORIAL
> NO REMEMBERED NAME—
> THEY HAVE PERISHED
> AS THOUGH THEY HAD NEVER BEEN.

All those life-giving women—

> STRONG—UPPITY—ANGRY—BEAUTIFUL—ABUSED
> RIGHTEOUS—DEPENDENT—ASSERTIVE—COWED
> AND USED.

With their bodies, most gave birth—

> AND WE ARE THEIR CHILDREN.
> WE SHARE THEIR LEGACIES
> FOR WE ARE THE HEIRS
> OF ALL THE AGES.

Their bodies are buried—

> BUT THEY ARE NOT FORGOTTEN
> THEIR LIVES SHALL NOT BE BLOTTED OUT.

For we know their wisdom—

> THEIR FEARS
> THEIR DREAMS
> THEIR SONGS
> THEIR LOVE.

We sing praises to famous women—

> WE SING THEIR PRAISES
> WE SING THEIR PRAISES.

Blessed Be.

mb

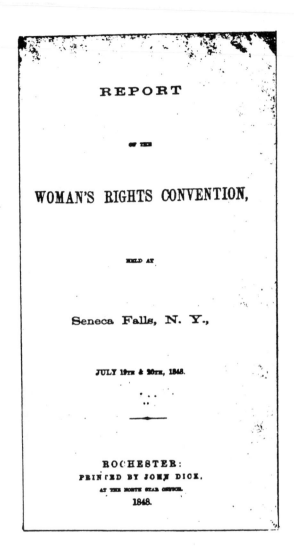

REPORT

OF THE

WOMAN'S RIGHTS CONVENTION,

HELD AT

Seneca Falls, N. Y.,

JULY 19TH & 20TH, 1848.

ROCHESTER:
PRINTED BY JOHN DICK,
AT THE NORTH STAR OFFICE.
1848.

The feminist movement is born in America: the front page of the *Report of the Woman's Rights Convention* at Seneca Falls, N.Y. *library of Congress. (Issuers of the Call for the Seneca Falls Convention of 1848)*

Spirit of Life

© February 1981 Surtsey Publishing
Words & music by Carolyn McDade

Spirit of Life
   Come to unto me
Sing in my heart
   All the stirrings of compassion
Blow in the wind
   Rise in the sea
Move in the hand
   Giving life the shape of justice
Roots hold me close
   Wings set me free
Spirit of Life
   Come to me—Come to me.

susan b. anthony 1820—1906

Susan B. Anthony read with great interest everything published in her village newspaper on the Seneca Falls conference. Most of the Resolutions—better education for women, equal pay, the right of women to free speech on public platforms—she approved, but when she read the radical Resolution calling for the right to vote, she laughed. The idea of women voting was absolutely. . . ridiculous.

However, when Susan met Elizabeth Cady Stanton in 1850 they quickly became the best of friends, spending the rest of their lives working together for women's rights—including the vote.

Anthony bore the brunt of traveling and lecturing, enduring hostility, ridicule, extreme cold and heat, bedbugs and miserable food. The 19th Amendment which finally gave women the franchise in 1920 is known as the Susan B. Anthony Amendment.

In thought and sympathy we were one, and in the division of labor we exactly complemented each other. . . While she is slow and analytical in composition, I am rapid and synthetic. I am the better writer, she the better critic. She supplied the facts and statistics, I the philosophy and rhetoric.

—Elizabeth Cady Stanton
Eighty Years and More

If Lucretia Mott typified the moral force of the movement, if Lucy Stone was its most gifted orator and Mrs. Stanton its outstanding philosopher, Susan Anthony was its incomparable organizer, who gave it force and direction for half a century.

—Eleanor Flexner,
Century of Struggle, 1959

PART I

Seneca Falls
—1848—

PROLOGUE

Four women (MARY ANN McCLINTOCK, MARTHA WRIGHT, JANE HUNT and LUCRETIA MOTT) stand in front of the set and read*; or, one by one, women step out to address the audience with a spot light on the speaker while the rest are in a 'freeze' position.

MARY ANN McCLINTOCK:
In the early days of the nineteenth century NO colleges were open to women, NO high schools. A few private schools taught the three "R's", and some "accomplishments" to the daughters of the rich. The poor went without learning until a later time when SOME girls were allowed to go to school during the summer months when the boys worked on the farm.

MARTHA WRIGHT:
THINKING women - women who were just beginning to have their consciousness' raised - were constantly irked by these limitations.

JANE HUNT:
In 1840 Elizabeth Cady, brilliant scholar and public speaker, daughter of a New York judge, married Henry Stanton. For their honeymoon, they sailed to London to attend the World Anti-Slavery Convention.

LUCRETIA MOTT:
My name is Lucretia Mott. I also attended this convention - as an accredited delegate. When we women from the United States presented our credentials the convention was thrown into an uproar and they refused to seat us. We were implored to be "ladylike" and not force the issue. We refused to withdraw.

---

*Caution readers to look at person speaking and NOT down at their script.

MARY ANN McCLINTOCK:

After a fierce argument, the men finally voted to exclude us women, but it was agreed we could attend meetings if we sat in the balcony, behind a screen - in a curtained enclosure - and be quiet. In protest, William Lloyd Garrison sat with us.

MARTHA WRIGHT:

After the meeting, Luretia Mott and Elizabeth Cady Stanton walked the streets of London enraged at the indignities and humiliation forced upon them because they were women. They decided that if women wanted to fight slavery or any other wrong, they would first have to win freedom for themselves. Then and there they resolved to call a women's rights conference and state their case to the world.

(Lucretia Mott exits RT behind the set).

JANE HUNT:

When Elizabeth Cady Stanton arrived back in the United States she started having babies - eventually seven in all - and it was not until 1848 that Lucretia Mott and Elizabeth Cady Stanton got together again. My name is Jane Hunt, Mrs. Richard Hunt, and they met in our home in Waterloo, New York.

PART II:

DRAMA

NO CURTAIN:
Jane points to set. Mary Ann McClintock stands by Martha Wright who sits in a parlor chair and starts to knit. Jane Hunt walks to "window" Stage LFT, and looks out.
CURTAIN:
As curtain rises, Martha Wright is sitting on a chair knitting, and Mary Ann McClintock stands by her chair. They are houseguests, as is Lucretia Mott who enters Stage RT, as if from another room. Jane Hunt is looking out the window, Stage LFT.

LUCRETIA MOTT:
(entering from RT)
Hasn't Elizabeth arrived yet? I am so eager to see her again. We have corresponded regularly, but I just can't believe we haven't seen one another in eight years—not since the summer we attended the Anti-Slavery Convention in London.

MARY ANN McCLINTOCK:
She is late.

JANE HUNT:
Here she is now and she looks wonderful!
(rushes to open the door)

ELIZABETH STANTON:
(entering from LFT)
Jane, I am so glad to see you.

JANE HUNT:
Welcome to my home.

ELIZABETH STANTON:
(as Jane takes her light wrap)
You don't know how delighted I was to receive your invitation.
(seeing Lucretia)
Lucretia!

(Elizabeth and Lucretia greet one another warmly. They embrace and are deeply moved; Elizabeth takes both of Lucretia's hands in hers.)

JANE HUNT:
(to Elizabeth)
Elizabeth, you know Lucretia's sister, Martha Wright. Martha is also my houseguest.

ELIZABETH STANTON:
Martha, so good to see you again.
(looking at knitting)
Something for the little one?
(laughs)

(Lucretia sits on couch)

JANE HUNT:
And you know Mary Ann McClintock. Elizabeth McClintock will join us later.

(The two women nod a greeting and Jane sits at tea table, pours a cup of tea and serves Mary Ann.)

ELIZABETH STANTON:
Hello, Mary.

LUCRETIA MOTT:
(to Elizabeth Stanton)
Lizzie, sit here by my side. Does thee know that I feel this is a momentous occasion? Something always happens when thee meets with me.

ELIZABETH STANTON:
(sitting beside Lucretia)
Something MUST come out of this meeting today. Somethig to help the condition of women. Have you heard what is happening to our good friend, Sarah Green?

JANE HUNT:
No, what is happening to her?

MARY ANN McCLINTOCK:
Please tell.

ELIZABETH STANTON:
Why, her husband, George, who is known as a worthy leader in his church, uses a horse whip on Sarah every few weeks, because HE claims she scolds too much.

JANE HUNT:
(serving tea to Elizabeth)

How brutal! Why doesn't Sarah do something to stop him?

ELIZABETH STANTON:

We have MAN-made laws which give George the right to beat Sarah and she can do NOTHING about it.

LUCRETIA MOTT:

No. Sarah can only take the thrashing. The same could happen to any of us.

(all are silent)

ELIZABETH STANTON:

Sarah can do nothing about it alone but together we CAN do something about the injustices women are suffering in this so-called land of freedom. I am sick at heart of our inferior status.

MARY ANN McCLINTOCK:
(putting her cup and saucer back on tea table)

But Elizabeth, what can we do to remedy our position? and these kinds of injustices?

ELIZABETH STANTON:

We must take action. We must foment a rebellion. We have waited too long. The Bill of Rights gives us the basic freedom of speech, the right to assemble, and the right to petition for grievances. We must start a movement. We'll call a convention. At the convention we'll cite these truths from the Declaration of Independence:
(stands, puts tea cup on table and reads:)

"We hold these truths to be self-evident, that all men" - and we'll add AND WOMEN "are created equal; that they are endowed with certain inalienable rights - that to secure these rights, governments are instituted, deriving their just powers from the consent of the governed". Then we'll add: "to prove this, let facts be submitted to a candid world."

JANE HUNT:

Oh, Elizabeth Cady Stanton, how could thee think of all those fine things?

ELIZABETH STANTON:

I have thought of little else for years and years. During the past few months, my thoughts have finally come together. Yes, after the preamble we'll list our grievances. We can have 18 of them just as our founding fathers had.

MARTHA WRIGHT:
We have more than that number, Elizabeth.

ELIZABETH STANTON:
You are right, Martha, we have many more.

LUCRETIA MOTT:
Suppose we call our demands the *Declaration of Sentiments?*

JANE HUNT:
I like that name.

MARY ANN McCLINTOCK:
Lucretia, that sounds good.

MARTHA WRIGHT:
Good!

ELIZABETH STANTON:
What if after we have listed our grievances we close our demands with these words:
(reads)
"Now in view of the disfranchisement of one-half of the people of this country, we insist that they have immediate admission to all the rights and privileges which belong to them as citizens of the United States."

JANE HUNT:
Oh, Elizabeth, what a fuss THAT will make! When will we have this conference, Elizabeth?

ELIZABETH STANTON:
When do you return to your home in Philadelphia, Lucretia?

LUCRETIA MOTT:
I leave next Friday.

ELIZABETH STANTON:
Lucretia, you are accustomed to speaking in public. We simply MUST have you with us. Shall we call the convention for next Wednesday and Thursday? July 19th and 20th?

LUCRETIA MOTT:
Oh, yes! And the meetings will surely require two days.

ELIZABETH STANTON:
We can have the convention in Seneca Falls. I'll arrange for it just as soon as I get home. Now, we must send out a call for the conference. Mary, be sure that our friend, Frederick Douglass, prints a notice in *The North Star.* I'll see that it gets into the *Seneca County Courier.* And we must make a list of grievances TODAY.

Jane, will you send messengers around to your friends here in Waterloo and ask them to bring in their grievances today?

JANE HUNT:
Yes, I'll go right away.

(Jane exits RT to another part of the house. She moves back Stage to LFT as she will soon enter LFT Stage with Antoinette Brown, Elizabeth W. McClintock, and Emily Peterson. Jane may exit LFT/Front door.)

LUCRETIA MOTT:
This is so very critical. We can't afford to make mistakes in this first women's rights convention. We must be very careful!

ELIZABETH STANTON:
The reason I was late in arriving today was because I was writing a call before I left home.
(giving paper to Mary Ann McClintock)
Mary, will you read it?

MARY ANN McCLINTOCK:
(Reads slowly)
"Women's Rights Convention - A convention to discuss the social, civil, and religious condition and rights of women will be held in the Wesleyan Chapel at Seneca Falls, New York, on Wednesday and Thursday, the 19th and 20th of July current, commencing at 10 o'clock a.m. During the first day the meeting will be exclusively for women, who are earnestly invited to attend. The public generally are invited to be present on the second day, when Lucretia Mott, of Philadelphia, and other ladies and gentlemen will address the convention."

MARTHA WRIGHT:
That sounds right to me. And I want to be the first to list a grievance!

ELIZABETH STANTON:
What is the wrong that you wish to name, Martha?

MARTHA WRIGHT:
It is this. When a woman marries she loses everything she possesses to her husband. All the beautiful quilts and linens that she has made for her use, her trousseau, her wedding presents, the very clothes she wears during the wedding ceremony, even her wedding ring. It all becomes **his** the minute she becomes **his** bride.

-257-

MARY ANN McCLINTOCK:
Yes, under Common Law a married woman has no rights. If she has property with the deed recorded in her name, she can't collect one penny of the income from such property without the consent of her husband. She can't even make a will to dispose of the property at her death. Surely we can do something to correct these wrongs.

ELIZABETH STANTON:
Yes, these are indeed grievous wrongs. Mary, will you write down a list of the grievances as they are given?

MARY ANN McCLINTOCK:
Yes, and that makes two of them.
(She takes out a pad and pen and quickly starts writing. If a desk is used, Mary sits at desk.)

LUCRETIA MOTT:
I want to add a grievance. When a married woman works for wages, every cent she makes can be taken from her by her husband . . . and legally.

ELIZABETH STANTON:
In addition, he can spend it **any way he chooses.**

LUCRETIA MOTT:
And we know he often spends it on drink for himself and **not** for the good of the children or the wife who earned the money in the first place.

MARTHA WRIGHT:
Let me name another injustice. Legally, the children belong to the husband. He may even will them away from the mother at his death, even an unborn baby, and the mother who bears the children must submit to this injustice. In the case of divorce, the children remain with the father no matter what his character may be; for he is their **legal** guardian. These laws should not exist in a civilized land! We must unite, we must rise up, we must demand that these injustices be corrected!

LUCRETIA MOTT:
(walking toward the window)
Thee are right, Martha. It is time. It is time.
(looking out window)
Oh, here comes Jane with some of thy friends.

(Jane enters bringing in Elizabeth W. McClintock, Antoinette Brown and Emily Peterson.)

JANE HUNT:
Hello, I'm sorry to be so detained.
(to Elizabeth Stanton, Lucretia and Martha)
I want thee to meet Elizabeth McClintock, Mary Ann's sister-in-law. Elizabeth is deeply interested in the removal of obstacles against women in this land.
(Elizabeth steps forward to shake hands or bows to seated cast)
And this is Antoinette Brown who works with Lucy Stone. And here is Emily Peterson who rails against the double standard in moral codes.
(to the women who have just entered)
Friends, thee know Mary and Martha. And this is Lucretia Mott, friend of Elizabeth Stanton.

ALL:
(Take time for women to greet one another with "Hello"—"Welcome"—"How are you?"—"Good to see you again"—"So glad you could come." Women scatter on stage)

JANE HUNT:
We have asked thee here today to list some of thy grievances.

ELIZABETH STANTON:
Yes, we have decided to hold the first women's rights convention next Wednesday and Thursday.

MARY ANN McCLINTOCK:
We are making a list of grievances. Antoinette, can you give us one on education?

ANTOINETTE BROWN:
Gladly. Yes, indeed, I am most upset.
(she steps center stage)
Custom has made it sufficient for girls to learn only the three "R's" so that they can read recipes for cooking, write to their parents when they marry and leave home, and to add up accounts in the homes of their husbands. There is **not one** high school for girls in all of these United States. Recently, Oberlin College has opened its doors to women, but even so they discriminate against them. Did you know that women students can study only a few subjects, like literature? In addition, they are required to clean up the men student's rooms, wash the men's clothing, serve the men at dinner and quietly listen to the men's orations. Why, when Lucy Stone graduated there last year she was not allowed to read her own

graduation essay. She was told that it would unsex her to read it before a mixed audience, that one of the professors would read it for her! Lucy replied that she would read it or nobody would. Therefore, it was never read. I plead for full education for females!

ELIZABETH W. McCLINTOCK:
(stepping center stage)
Mary, I plead for women to be permitted to enter the medical profession. Women and children should have women doctors to treat them. Women would make wonderful doctors—after all, they are the ancient healers. Will you please see that women be allowed to become doctors?

EMILY PETERSON:
(to Mary McClintock who is busily writing)
My name is Emily Peterson. I have come to ask you to do what you can to have in our society only one moral code. The same for men **and** women. Just as long as society accepts immorality in men we have lax morals. Ladies, will you please do something about this code? This double standard code?
(walks to Jane Hunt who is seated at the tea table)
Thank you, Jane.

JANE HUNT:
(very seriously)
No, thank YOU. Thank YOU for coming.

(the three women visitors prepare to leave)

MARY ANN McCLINTOCK:
There is so much to do!

ELIZABETH McCLINTOCK:
Thee can meet at my house tomorrow.

MARTHA WRIGHT:
Good. We'll be there early in the morning.
(as the three women visitors exit left)
Thank you, Elizabeth—and Antoinette, and Emily.

ALL:
(ad lib with 'goodbye' and 'thank you' as the women exit out the front door.)

(NOTE: If one of these women also plays the role of Sally Bridges, she will now make appropriate costume change.)

ELIZABETH STANTON:

I can't wait any longer. I must list a grievance which I feel is of the utmost importance. Women must have access to the ballot. They MUST be permitted to vote. Not until women have the power of the ballot will they have the power to correct these abuses against women. I will demand the vote for women and I will base my demand on taxation. Our forefathers won their rights with the slogan "Taxation without representation is Tyranny!" Surely the world will realize that the principle applies to women as well as to men.

LUCRETIA MOTT:
(walking toward sofa)
Why, Lizzie, thee will not dare! Thee will make us look ridiculous. We must go slowly. And besides, thee will SPOIL all our plans if thee makes THAT demand.
(sits on sofa next to Elizabeth Stanton)

ELIZABETH STANTON:
No, I will not. You will see, Lucretia.
(slowly)
The power to make the laws is the right through which we can secure ALL OTHER RIGHTS.

JANE HUNT:
(walking toward window—left)
I don't know, Elizabeth. Most everyone thinks that women's brains are too soft to understand politics. I just don't know. . .
(looks out window)

MARTHA WRIGHT:
I agree with Elizabeth. Women must secure to themselves the elected franchise. It is our sacred right. It is our duty. . .

JANE HUNT:
(interrupting)
Oh, I see Sally Bridges coming!

(Sally knocks and Jane opens the door)
Hello, Sally. Thee are well? Thy children?

SALLY BRIDGES:
They are well, Mrs. Hunt. I had your message awhile ago and I am here to plead with you to try to make it possible for women to share

the easy jobs with men.

(pause)

I mean, there are few jobs that women are allowed and they are all hard ones. I take in washing for a living. Really.

(speaking slowly)

I am a widow with five children and I have to bend over the wash tub all day long to make enough money to feed my children. Men have all the good jobs and they will not share them with women. I ask you, is it right for men to keep us from having better jobs? Well, that's all I have to say. I have to go now. Goodbye.

(Sally exits)

ELIZABETH STANTON:

Now THAT wrong will surely prod us on to work for rights for women. How many grievances are there on the list now, Mary?

MARY ANN McCLINTOCK:

(counting)

That makes seventeen.

ELIZABETH STANTON:

Lucretia, don't you have another grievance to name?

LUCRETIA MOTT:

Yes. All of thee know how I have always been concerned about religious matters. Thee know, of course, that I am a Quaker. It is my feeling that men have usurped the perogative of Jehovah himself in claiming their right to assign to woman her sphere of action. Why should only men run the churches? Women have the right to choose their place in the church as well as elsewhere. I ask that woman be given this right.

MARTHA WRIGHT:

I agree with Lucretia.

ELIZABETH STANTON:

I am sure all of us agree with her. That makes our eighteen Sentiments. I am willing to go before the convention with them. Do you all agree?

ALL:

(All ad lib agreement—except Lucretia—who keeps quiet)

ELIZABETH STANTON:

Do you feel this way about the Sentiments, Lucretia?

LUCRETIA MOTT:

Yes, I do, Lizzie, all of them except thine. I do NOT feel that we should demand the ballot. Women voting will be thought of as. . . ridiculous.

ELIZABETH STANTON:

Now, now, Lucretia. Our hands are tied until we can vote. I must start for home.

(rising)

Friends, in a few days we must be prepared for the first woman's rights convention ever held anywhere in the world.

MARY ANN McCLINTOCK:

This is a tremendous task for us to undertake.

(Jane Hunt picks up Elizabeth's shawl and gives it to her.)

ELIZABETH STANTON:

Yes, Mary, it is, but meet me in Seneca Falls on Wednesday and we'll start to remove mountains of grievances.

LUCRETIA MOTT:

(standing as Stanton exits)

We'll meet thee there with mustard seeds of faith and we'll remove the mountains. We'll win the victory. . .SOME DAY.

CURTAIN (or exit)

PART III

Postscript

Elizabeth W. McClintock, Antoinette Brown and Emily Peterson enter and stand center stage. As each woman addresses the audience, she may step forward (use a spotlight on her as other women are in a 'freeze' position), or women look at woman who is speaking (NOT down at their script).

ELIZABETH McCLINTOCK:
Wednesday morning, July 19, 1848 came. Armed with their Declaration of Sentiments, their resolutions, and an armful of law books for reference, these pioneer women converged on Wesleyan Chapel in Seneca Falls, New York where they found a crowd assembled—and the door locked.

ANTOINETTE BROWN:
A young student, Mrs. Stanton's nephew, was hoisted to a window through which he entered and opened the door. It was found that no woman had ever presided over a meeting. In a hurried conference it was decided to ask a man to take charge of the convention. So, John Mott, tall and dignified in his Quaker attire, called the meeting to order, and the Women's Rights Movement— the Women's Liberation Movement—was launched.

EMILY PETERSON:
Lucretia Mott, accustomed to speaking to the Society of Friends, stated the object of the meeting. A young lawyer read a series of the most exasperating laws against women. Elizabeth Cady Stanton read the Declaration of Sentiments. Yes, including the controversial resolution of women having the right to vote. All resolutions were offered and all passed unanimously—except for women having the right to vote. But the resolution asking for the right to vote DID PASS.

ELIZABETH McCLINTOCK:
The convention issued a ringing declaration of women's rights which stated that all men AND WOMEN are created equal.

ANTOINETTE BROWN:
The convention caused a nationwide commotion. Newspapers carried the news on the front pages. Except for two or three papers the press was bitter against the movement. They ridiculed the

women and their supporters unmercifully. The country resounded with denunciations.

EMILY PETERSON:
On Sunday, ministers in their pulpits heaped ridicule and derision upon the meeting. So intense was the disfavor that almost all of the one hundred men and women who had signed the resolutions withdrew their names. Disapproval from the pulpit, sarcasm and ridicule are powerful forces for conformity. Frederick Douglass, however, remained a faithful friend to women's rights and supported a follow-up meeting to be held two weeks later at the Unitarian Church in Rochester, New York.

ELIZABETH McCLINTOCK:
Some women insisted that a woman preside. Abigail Bush, a Quaker, was elected president. Lucretia Mott, Mary Ann McClintock and Elizabeth Stanton did not keep pace with their constituents this time—for they were so opposed to the idea of a woman presiding that they threatened to walk out of the meeting.*

ANTOINETTE BROWN:
However, when the day of the meeting arrived. Abigail Bush was equal to her duties. In her opening speech she began:
(Slowly)
"Friends, we present ourselves here before you with trembling frames and faltering tongues—but we trust that you will bear with our weakness in the infancy of the movement."

EMILY PETERSON:
Abigail's competence completely won over Elizabeth who, ashamed and embarrassed, resolved "Never again will I suggest that women are incapable of any public task!"

ELIZABETH McCLINTOCK:
And so began the women's movement, a most remarkable force for social change. To Lucretia Mott, Elizabeth wrote: "The publicity given to our ideas. . . will start women thinking and men too; and when men and women think about a new question, the first step in progress is taken."

A woman to preside at a meeting at that time was a striking innovation; they called it "a most hazardous experiment."

ANTOINETTE BROWN:
It took 72 years and 87 separate campaigns for the feminist crusade to win the vote in 1920. Of the 260 women and 40 men who attended the convention, only one, Charlotte Woodward, lived to see women vote.

EMILY PETERSON:
In 1963 the Equal Pay Act passed and in 1964 Martha Wright Griffiths wrote the anti-sex discrimination clause into the Civil Rights Act. Then, in 1973, with the Supreme Court decision in Roe -vs- Wade, we gained a basic and crucial right—control over our bodies. And now, books, films, and international conferences are spreading feminist ideas throughout the world.

ELIZABETH McCLINTOCK:
Long live the memory of Lucretia Mott and Elizabeth Cady Stanton and ALL our foremothers who paved the way!
(To cast)
FOREMOTHERS, come forward and take a bow!

Cast comes forward and curtsies.

(END)

Helmer: Remember - before all else you are a wife and mother.

Nora: I don't believe that anymore. I believe that before all else I am a human being - just as you are.

-Henrik Ibsen

OPTIONAL ENDINGS

Optional Ending #1:

As applause dies down, Elizabeth Cady Stanton and Lucretia Mott step forward to lead a discussion with the audience.

ELIZABETH CADY STANTON:
Now friends, at the age of 86 I left this earth in Nineteen-ought-two. Please tell me what has happened since then. Did we do any good? Does the world remember us?

LUCRETIA MOTT:
I left this world in 1880—over 100 years ago. How is it now with women? What issues need to be addressed? Who are thy leaders now? How is it with thee?

Optional Ending #2:

As applause dies down, a feminist* in jeans and tee-shirt rushes center stage carrying a picket/demonstration sign (current issue) and loudly interjects:

MODERN FEMINIST:
Yes we've come a long way, Foremothers, BUT we still have a long way to go. We don't have:

★ comparable worth or pay equity

★ enough women in Congress or state legislatures or county and city governments

★ enough women in the pulpits/university professors/doctors. . .

★ paid maternity leaves

*Modern feminist can be the woman who played the role of Mary Ann McClintock, Elizabeth Cady Stanton, Lucretia Mott or Martha Wright who has done a quick costume change.

★ adequate access to health care

★ guaranteed child support

★ elimination of double standards in morals, or social and marital practices

★ gender inclusive language

★ protection from rape/molestation/incest/sexual harassment

★ adequate income for older women

★ enough shelters for battered women

Modern Feminist selects several issues and initiates discussion with audience. Cast can join in, too.

The First Woman's Rights Convention

The convention, which was held two days in the Methodist Church, was in every way a grand success. The house was crowded at every session, the speaking good, and a religious earnestness dignified all the proceedings.

These were the hasty initiative steps of "the most momentous reform that had yet been launched on the world—the first organized protest against the injustice which had brooded for ages over the character and destiny of one-half the race." No words could express our astonishment on finding, a few days afterward, that what seemed to us so timely, so rational, and so sacred, should be a subject for sarcasm and ridicule to the entire press of the nation. With our Declaration of Rights and Resolutions for a text, it seemed as if every man who could wield a pen prepared a homily on "woman's sphere." All the journals from Maine to Texas seemed to strive with each other to see which could make our movement appear the most ridiculous. The anti-slavery papers stood by us manfully and so did Frederick Douglass, both in the convention and in his paper, *The North Star*, but so pronounced was the popular voice against us, in the parlor, press, and pulpit, that most of the ladies who had attended the convention and signed the declaration, one by one, withdrew their names and influence and joined our persecutors. Our friends gave us the cold shoulder and felt themselves disgraced by the whole proceeding.

If I had the slightest premonition of all that was to follow that convention, I fear I should not have had the courage to risk it, and I must confess that it was with fear and trembling that I consented to attend another, one month afterward, in Rochester.

—Elizabeth Cady Stanton:
Eighty Years and More
Reminiscences 1815 - 1897
(Schocken Books 1898/1971) p.149

"Elizabeth Cady Stanton and Reverence for Trees"
Sermon Brief—January 6, 1985

. . . Elizabeth Cady Stanton was remarkable! And, she was right about herself. She did grow more radical as she grew older. Determined, feisty, dedicated, articulate and energetic, she was the dominant force in the women's movement of the 19th century.

She believed fervently in women's self-reliance and independence and late in life she expressed her view in an essay titled, "The Solitude of Self." And yet she was sustained throughout her life by friends like Lucretia Mott and Susan B. Anthony. It was not a tragic individualism she espoused because she had a large soul. In writing about the women who organized the 1848 Seneca Falls conference, she said, "they had souls large enough to feel the wrongs of others."

And, I believe that is what it ultimately comes down to as we struggle to become better people. How large is your soul? Who do I include in my living and loving and who do I exclude? Stanton had a soul large enough to feel the wrongs of others.

What voices shall we listen to? What voices summon us by example to enlarge our own souls? Elizabeth Cady Stanton is one such voice for me.

Here's a word of challenge from Stanton to all men, something to ponder for it says much: "Men as a general rule have very little reverence for trees."

And, a word for the women: "The ignorance and indifference of the majority of women as to their status as citizens is not remarkable, for history shows that the masses of all oppressed classes, in the most degraded conditions, have been stolid and apathetic until partial success had crowned the faith and the enthusiasm of the few."

And, for all of us, women and men alike: May we all grow more radical the older we become.

—Rev. Bruce Southworth

**M
A
R
C
H
8**

INTERNATIONAL WOMEN'S DAY

International Women's Day—March 8

The second International Conference of Socialist Women, held in Copenhagen in 1910, adopted Clara Zetkin's proposal that March 8 be set aside as International Women's Day—a holiday to commemorate the 1908 strike of 40,000 poor seamstresses protesting sweatshop working conditions in New York's Lower East Side and demanding decent housing and the right to vote.

Over the years, March 8th has brought tens of thousands of European working women into the streets to demand peace, decent jobs, protection for pregnant workers, the right to vote and the right to organize labor unions.

Today, in socialist and other countries throughout the world, there are speeches and editorials reviewing the long struggle for women's rights, and women receive flowers, books and other small gifts, are granted a day off from work and taken out to dinner.

International Women's Day is more than our traditional Mother's Day and it is increasingly becoming popular in the United States often coinciding with activities such as Women's Day In The Park and Women's History Week activities.

Frederick Douglass

FREDERICK DOUGLASS 1817—1895

Abolitionist and former slave asked to take part in the Seneca Falls Convention of 1848. He eloquently 'saved the day' by persuading participants to adopt the Woman's Suffrage Resolution. The masthead of his weekly newspaper contained the legend "Right is of no sex."

"Frederick Douglass"
Sermon Brief—February 23, 1986

"Those who profess to favor freedom, and yet deprecate agitation, are people who want crops without plowing up the ground."
—Frederick Douglass

. . . One small incident reflects the temperament of this—perhaps the greatest agitator for black equality. In the last decade of his life, at age 70, Frederick Douglass and his wife were travelling in Europe and decided to visit Egypt as well. Douglass decided to climb to the top of the Great Pyramid, 470 feet above the base, and he did just that. We shall never know all he thought and felt, but part of my image of this freedom fighter includes a picture of him surveying the world from this lofty perch.

The life of Frederick Douglass was one of divine discontent; he was the kind of person that Martin Luther King, Jr. would years later call 'creatively maladjusted.'

His agitation did not focus on the plight of his people alone. He was an ardent feminist and it was he who in 1848 at the Seneca Falls conference helped to secure the passage of the 9th and most controversial resolution proposed by Elizabeth Cady Stanton and her friends, namely the article calling for the right of women to vote. Douglass seconded the motion and argued for it eloquently; most women present were against such a motion, saying it went too far and would make them look silly. Yet, after Douglass spoke it carried by a small margin. . .

Unfortunately, sometimes agitation is deplored; sometimes it is easier to allow the comforts of the world, the seductions of the world, and our own personal heartaches and pains to inure us to the ancient call to do justice.

Let me close with just one final thought about the example to us in the life of Frederick Douglass. Throughout his life he had a vision of what life could be, how it might be. He suffered defeats, quite literally life-threatening beatings, yet he would always return with his head high and his vision exceeding his immediate grasp. I like to think about Frederick Douglass, ex-slave, orator, writer and agitator, at age 70 sitting and resting on top of the Great Pyramid. And, I take particular delight in knowing that his final home on a hillside across the Anacostia River from Washington, D.C., this fine home, an estate, owned by this wonderful man, an ex-slave, had once belonged to none other than Robert E. Lee.

What a strange and wonderful world this is. What wonderous and good things we too may yet do, this day and every day.

—Rev. Bruce Southworth

*William
Lloyd Garrison*

WILLIAM LLOYD GARRISON 1805—1879

Garrison urged delegates to the World Anti-Slavery Convention
(London, 1840) to allow female participation. Even though he was
eager to address the Convention, when women were denied the
right to be seated he protested by joining them in the balcony where
they were forced to sit behind a curtain.

He said: "After battling so many long years for the liberties of
Africans. . . I can take no part in a Convention that strikes down
the most sacred rights of all women."

SONG:

"America, the Even More Beautiful"
(Sung to the tune of "America The Beautiful")

Oh Beautiful, for freedom's sake,
   the bright new world to be
With men and women living there
   In full equality
America, America, your daughters long to see
That all thy good is PEOPLEHOOD
   From sea to shining sea

Oh beautiful, for girls to grow
   As strong and free as boys,
With all of life available
   In free and equal choice
America, America, your daughters long to see
That all thy good is PEOPLEHOOD
   From sea to shining sea

Two hundred years we've served the land
   And waited for the day,
Your promise made,
   Fulfilled at last by ERA.
America, America, your daughters long to see
That all thy good is PEOPLEHOOD
   From sea to shining sea.

SONG:

WE MIGHT COME IN A FIGHTING [*]

By Carolyn McDade

Well, we might come in a-fighting,
   Cause there's lots that needs a-righting;
We've learned a lot from living
   Never taught to us in schools;
If they say come in like a man,
   Well they must not understand,
When we enter in the game,
   We're gonna change the godamned rules.

Well, they say if you enter in a man's world,
   There's got to be a boss,
Someone a-giving orders,
   Or it'll end in a total loss;
But we know just from living
   That all folks got stuff for giving,
Them hard lines of authority
   We're bound to step across.

There somehow is this feeling
   We've got to work from nine to five—
Cause that's what makes a person,
   Worthy to be alive,
Yet most of what they're doin'
   Is bringing the world to ruin,—
Let's speed up on the living
   And slow down on the drive. [**]

---

[*]"We Might Come In A-Fighting" is available on recording "Songs of Liberation" by the Arlington Women's Caucus, Rounder Records, 186 Willow Avenue, Someville, MA 02144. (#4006)

[**]See page 147 for music.